SHAKESPEARE'S Flowers in stumpwork

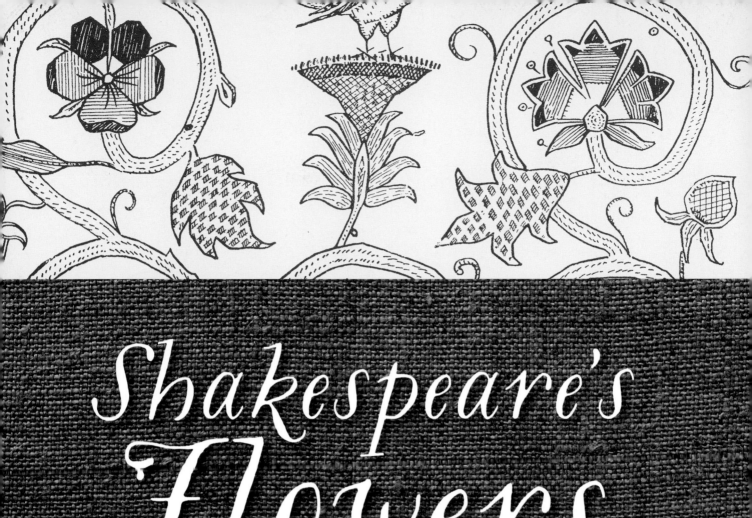

Shakespeare's Flowers

IN STUMPWORK

Jane Nicholas

SALLYMILNER
PUBLISHING

First published in 2015 by
Sally Milner Publishing Pty Ltd
734 Woodville Road
Binda NSW 2583 AUSTRALIA

© Jane Nicholas 2015

Design: Caroline Verity
Editing: Anne Savage
llustrations: Wendy Gorton
Photography: Tim Connolly
Printed in China

National Library of Australia Cataloguing-in-Publication entry:

Creator:	Nicholas, Jane, author.
Title:	Shakespeares flowers in stumpwork / Jane Nicholas.
ISBN:	9781863514811 (hardback)
Series:	Milner craft series.
Notes:	Includes bibliographical references.
Subjects:	Embroidery--Patterns.
	Stump work.
	Flowers in art.

Dewey Number: 746.44

10 9 8 7 6 5 4 3 2 1

I know a bank where the wild thyme blows,

Where oxlips and the nodding violet grows;

Quite over-canopied with luscious woodbine,

'With sweet musk-roses and with eglantine:

There sleeps Titania, sometime of the night,

Lull'd in these flowers with dances and delight ...

A Midsummer Night's Dream (ii.1)

Contents

Introduction

The era of Elizabeth I (1533–1603) and William Shakespeare (1564–1616), was a time of relative peace and tranquillity—conditions England had not experienced for centuries—which gave rise to an unprecedented period of growth. When Elizabeth ascended the throne in 1558, much of the land which had previously been held by the Church was in the hands of the aristocracy and an increasingly affluent middle class, who now found themselves in a position to spend more on pleasures and luxuries. This long period of stability saw not only a flourishing of the arts—music, literature and needlework—but also of gardens, gardeners and plant collectors. This was the beginning of the first English gardening craze. The upper classes had the land, they had the time, the disposable income, and their international trade and exploration was bringing back seeds and cuttings from the farthest reaches of the globe—marigolds from Mexico, apple, pear and apricot trees from France and the Netherlands, clematis from Italy and, by the 1570s, tulips, daffodils and hyacinths from Turkey, all of which expanded the already wide variety of imported seeds and plants available—Madonna lilies, lupins, snowdrops, cyclamen, hollyhocks, lily of the valley, peonies, ranunculus, anemones, polyanthus … the list was extensive. While gardens and plant collecting had always had a herbal and medicinal emphasis, flowers were now valued for pleasure's sake as well—for their intrinsic beauty, for their scents and for their rarity. The pleasure garden became an element of Elizabethan status.

Elizabethan gardens were usually laid out in formal, geometric designs, with knot gardens their most common feature. The knots, in square or rectangular patterns, were created by the use of one or more different types of plant, such as rosemary, lavender, thyme or clipped box. The lines of the knot were interlaced so that they appeared to weave in and out of each other. The spaces between the knots were filled with coloured sands, gravels or grasses to emphasise the overall pattern—especially when viewed from an overlooking terrace, window or gallery. Sometimes the enclosed beds contained fragrant herbs or flowers, such as primroses, violets, sweet Williams and gillyflowers.

The gardens of the period were generally enclosed in some way—by walls, hedges, fences or even moats—providing a measure of protection from prevailing winds (and wild animals) and a warmer microclimate. Plans of Elizabethan manor houses show walled gardens, often unconnected, and sometimes leading off from different rooms in the house. There were walled gardens for pleasure, for vegetables and medicinal herbs, while others had their walls covered in espaliered fruit trees. Apples, figs, plums, pears and vines were commonly grown against reflecting brick walls, which provided extra heat.

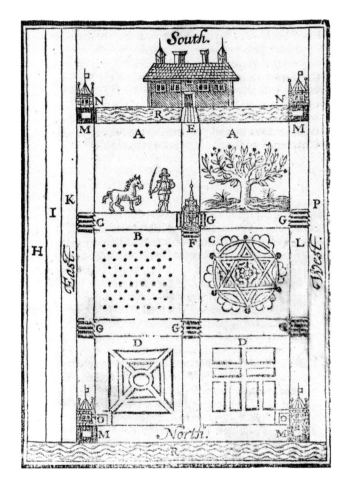

A plan for a typical manor-house garden in England, from William Lawson's New Orchard and Garden *(1618). It shows a garden, with a moat and river, divided into six sections, each of which is for separate garden features. In two there are topiary pieces and espaliered fruit trees, in another, fruit. An area is set aside for knots, and the remaining two sections are for vegetables.*

Flowers were valued for a variety of purposes: ceremonial, domestic and medicinal. Garlands of flowers played an important role in many occasions, adorning people on May Day celebrations and caskets at funerals.

Cut flowers, potted plants and strewn herbs were used to sweeten and beautify Elizabethan houses, as remarked upon by the Dutchman, Levinus Lemnius, on his travels in England in 1560:

their chambers and parlours strewed over with fresh herbes refreshed mee; their nosegays finely intermingled with sundry of fragraunt flowers, in their bed-chambers and privy rooms, with comfortable smell cheered me up, and entirely delighted all my senses.

In *The Country Housewife's Garden* of 1617, William Lawson describes how half of the lady's garden plot was given over to herbs and to flowers such as violets, pansies, daisies, nasturtiums, gillyflowers and marigolds for the making of garlands and nosegays (small bunches of mixed flowers—also called 'tussie mussies').

A wide range of native plants was used for medicinal purposes, and flowers and herbs provided the raw material for many perfumes. Marjoram, one of Queen Elizabeth's favourite herbs, was used to make 'Queen Elizabeth's Perfume'. The printed herbals that appeared in the sixteenth century, such as William Turner's *New Herbal*, published in 1548, were a result of the growing interest in gardening practice and the practical use of plants. In 1577, Thomas Hill launched the first actual gardening book ever written—*The Gardener's Labyrinth* (he wrote under the pseudonym of Didymus Mountaine).

A contemporary of Shakespeare, Hill summed up the gardening spirit of the age in one of his most famous passages:

The life of man in this world is but thraldom, when the Sences are not pleased and what rarer object can there be on earth ... than a beautifull and Odoriferous Garden plot Artificially composed, where he may read and contemplate on the wonderful works of the great Creator, in Plants and Flowers: for if he observeth with a judicial eye, and a serious judgement their variety of Colours, Sents, Beauty, Shapes, Interlacings, Enamilling, Mixture, Turnings, Windings, Embossments, Operations and Vertues, it is most admirable to behold and meditate upon the same.

Didymus Mountaine, THE GARDENER'S LABYRINTH (1577)

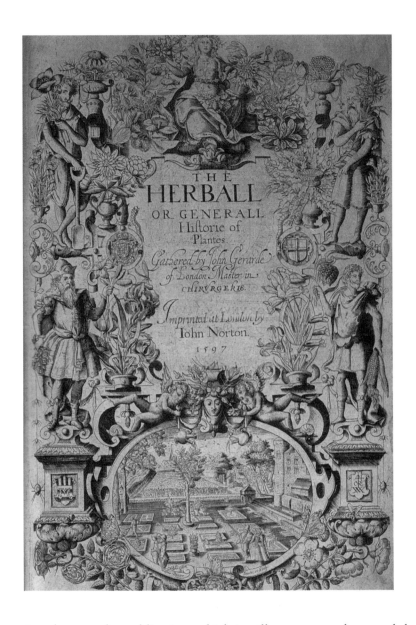

The title page of John Gerard's Herball or Generall Historie of Plantes, *published in 1597. It shows the goddess Flora holding 'White Mountaine Pinke', 'Lillie of the valley' and the common American sunflower. One male figure holds the 'Purple Passe flower' (*Anemone pulsatilla*), another holds the crown imperial, a third the Madonna lily and the fourth the 'Changeable chequered Daffodil' (*Fritillaria mcleagris*) and 'Turkie Wheat' (*Zea mays*). The garden in the cartouche is probably Lord Burghley's Theobalds, where Gerard worked.*

Another popular publication, which is still eminently readable today, was John Gerard's fully illustrated *Herball or Generall Historie of Plants* of 1597, in which he describes his collection of plants and their 'vertues' with special charm. He delighted in describing the colours and textures of the flowers, often borrowing terms from textiles and needlework for the purpose: he describes

There's rosemary, that's for remembrance;
pray, love, remember:
and there is pansies, that's for thoughts. Hamlet (iv.5)

the 'glosse like velvet' of the 'Floramor' (*Celosia argentea*), with its red and green leaves shaded like parrot feathers, and sunflowers, 'the middle whereof is made of unshorn velvet, or some curious cloth wrought with the needle'. Gerard, head gardener at Lord Burghley's Theobalds in London, had his own garden in Holburn, where he grew more than a thousand plants: 'all the rare simples' and 'all manner of strange trees, herbes, rootes, plants, flowers, and other such rare things' which he listed in his 1596 catalogue.

The medicinal properties and moral characteristics that herbals attributed to numerous plants contributed to their role in popular culture, as revealed in the literature of the time.

The Elizabethan era was also famous for the flourishing of English drama, led by playwrights such as William Shakespeare and Christopher Marlowe. While Shakespeare's extensive knowledge

on a variety of subjects, ranging from science to art, was evident in his work, his knowledge of plants and the beauty of nature stems from his life as a country man, not as a botanist.

His observations are taken directly from nature and are rich in the plant and herb lore of Tudor England, as observed, delightfully, by the Reverend T.S. Thistleton Dyer in 1883:

That Shakespeare possessed an extensive knowledge of the history and superstitions associated with flowers is evident, from even a slight perusal of his plays. Apart from the extensive use which he has made of these lovely objects of nature for the purpose of embellishing, or adding pathos to, passages here and there; he has also, with a master hand, interwoven many a little legend or superstition, thereby infusing an additional force into his writings.

T.F. Thistleton Dyer, FOLK-LORE OF SHAKESPEARE (1883)

12

In emerald tufts, flowers purple, blue and white;
Like sapphire, pearl, and rich embroidery,

The Merry Wives of Windsor (iv.5)

Shakespeare grew up in the small country town of Stratford-upon-Avon, leaving for London around 1585. It has been conjectured that John Gerard and Shakespeare were acquainted, and that Shakespeare may have seen Gerard's extensive garden.

Shakespeare became a successful dramatist, being a member of the Lord Chamberlain's company (which became the King's Company after the death of Elizabeth in 1603), and writing many popular plays for them. He prospered, regularly returning to his home and garden in Stratford, where he died in 1616.

In *Shakespeare's Flowers* (1994), Jenny de Gex discusses the way in which wild flowers, herbs and gardens are a recurrent feature throughout Shakespeare's work: from Oberon's 'bank where the wild thyme blows' and where oxlips, violets, woodbine, musk-roses and eglantine grow, together with a 'weed [fritillary] wide enough to wrap a fairy in' (*A Midsummer Night's Dream*), to

the Spring Song, 'when daisies pied, and violets blue', with lady-smocks and yellow cuckoo-buds 'do paint the meadows with delight'.

Perdita, in *A Winter's Tale*, talks of daffodils, violets and 'pale primroses', while in *Hamlet*, Ophelia drowns in the 'weeping brook', garlanded with 'crow-flowers, nettles, daisies and long purples'. Shakespeare used plants to symbolise 'yearning, unrequited love, passion, malice and mischief, joy, triumph and glory'.

Given the late sixteenth-century obsession with gardens and flower collecting, it is not surprising that a corresponding enthusiasm was reflected in the needlework of the time. Flowers were everywhere—on clothing and furnishings—worked in blackwork, whitework and all forms of polychrome silk embroidery—from surface stitchery, including needlelace, to floral slips in canvas work (stumpwork was not a feature of Elizabethan embroidery—it blossomed later,

Elizabethan sleeve-panel in blackwork; held in the Royal Scottish Museum, Edinburgh

in the middle of the seventeenth century). In the more affluent families, a girl's embroidery education was considered an essential—and refined—accomplishment. The chief skills of the ladies of Queen Elizabeth's court were fluency in Latin, Greek and modern languages, and proficiency in needlework, spinning and music.

Flowers and embroidery were very closely linked in the Elizabethan mind. In his dedication to Sir William Cecil in his *Herball*, John Gerard wrote:

For if delight may provoke men's labour, what greater delight is there than to behold the earth apparelled with plants, as with a robe of imbroidered works, set with orient pearles and garnished with great diversitie of rare and costly jewels.

Flowers, herbs, and plants in general, especially those introduced from far-off places, were of great fascination to sixteenth-century embroiderers. They loved them for their beauty and scent, were curious about their medicinal attributes, and were amused and charmed by inferences of symbolism.

Their embroideries, worked either in monochrome (blackwork) or coloured silks and metal threads, began to feature flowers such as the rose (a particular favourite, as white and red roses were also emblems of the now united houses of York and Lancaster), peonies, primroses, cowslips and eglantine, columbines, cornflowers, gillyflowers and pansies (Queen Elizabeth's favourite flower), borage, daffodils, snowdrops and bluebells, foxgloves, marigolds, violets and daisies, honeysuckle, irises, thistles and pea pods; fruits in the form of grapes, raspberries and strawberries; and acorns, oak, holly leaves and the pomegranate, an exotic addition. These flowers were worked either in sprig form or in a coiling floral patterning, known then as scrolls, but referred to today as *rinceaux*. This is a scroll of foliage that alternates in clockwise and counter-clockwise directions as it repeats in a linear arrangement.

It was by far the most popular design format in sixteenth- and early seventeenth-century English embroidery. The floral designs tended to be densely packed, with the spaces between the flowers filled with buds, tendrils and leaves, and insects such as bees, butterflies and caterpillars.

The projects in this book feature many of the flowers to be found in the gardens, fields and hedgerows of sixteenth-century England. The designs, inspired by the painted border of a letter written in the late sixteenth century and an embroidered panel from the early seventeenth century, have been worked in stumpwork and surface embroidery.

The embroidered *'Border of Shakespeare's Flowers'* was inspired by the painted border of a letter written by Lady Anne Clifford to her father in 1598. The border contains fourteen assorted flowers and fruits popular at the time, including the Apothecary rose, sweet briar and heartsease, barberries, bellflower, borage and periwinkle, cornflower, gillyflower and knapweed, and grapes, plums, redcurrants and strawberries.

The letter was introduced to me by Phillipa Turnbull, who requested that I interpret the flowers in the border in stumpwork for her Lady Anne's Needlework English Retreat and Scottish Tour in 2012. It was for this event that I designed and taught Sampler One, which features four of the flowers depicted in the border. Another eight flowers from the letter are contained in Samplers Two and Three. During this retreat, I had the privilege of viewing the original letter (held in a private collection) and its exquisite border of flowers, hand-painted in water-colour. A rare treat indeed!

The *'Elizabethan Flower Panel'* was inspired by an early seventeenth-century English embroidered panel, worked on linen in coloured silks and metal threads, held in the collection of the Embroiderers' Guild.

This design also features flowers popular in Elizabethan times—a primrose, bluebells, a crab apple and buds, the honeysuckle, pea pods, and a traditional red rose—all enclosed by coiling stems, whipped with gold thread. Nestled among the foliage can be found a bee, a plump caterpillar and a tiny ladybird.

The original panel was one of the pieces I was fortunate enough to have had the opportunity to study when I visited the Embroiderers' Guild at Hampton Court Palace in 1999, as part of my study tour with my Churchill Fellowship. I continue to be grateful for the knowledge and experiences that were facilitated by this award.

It has been a great pleasure to delve into the gardening craze of the sixteenth century, to return to the works of Shakespeare with an older eye, to have the excuse to read excerpts from Gerard's charming herbal yet again (it always makes me smile), and to have the excuse to revisit the glorious embroideries of the Elizabethan era—one of the greatest periods of English needlework.

A BORDER OF
Shakespeare's Flowers

PART ❧ ONE

A BORDER OF
SHAKESPEARE'S FLOWERS

This embroidered border was inspired by the painted border of a letter written by Lady Anne Clifford to her father in 1598—the time of Elizabeth I and Shakespeare.

Worked on ivory silk satin, in stumpwork and surface embroidery, this design features fourteen assorted flowers and fruits popular at the time, including the Apothecary rose, sweet briar and heartsease, barberries, bellflower, borage and periwinkle, cornflower, gillyflower and knapweed, and grapes, plums, redcurrants and strawberries. As in the original letter, the panel is outlined with pairs of fine red lines—these have been worked in back stitch.

This border may be used to surround a mirror, or to enclose a special photograph, a monogram, a precious memento, or perhaps a tiny stumpwork figure.

Opposite: not actual size (enlarged by 10%)

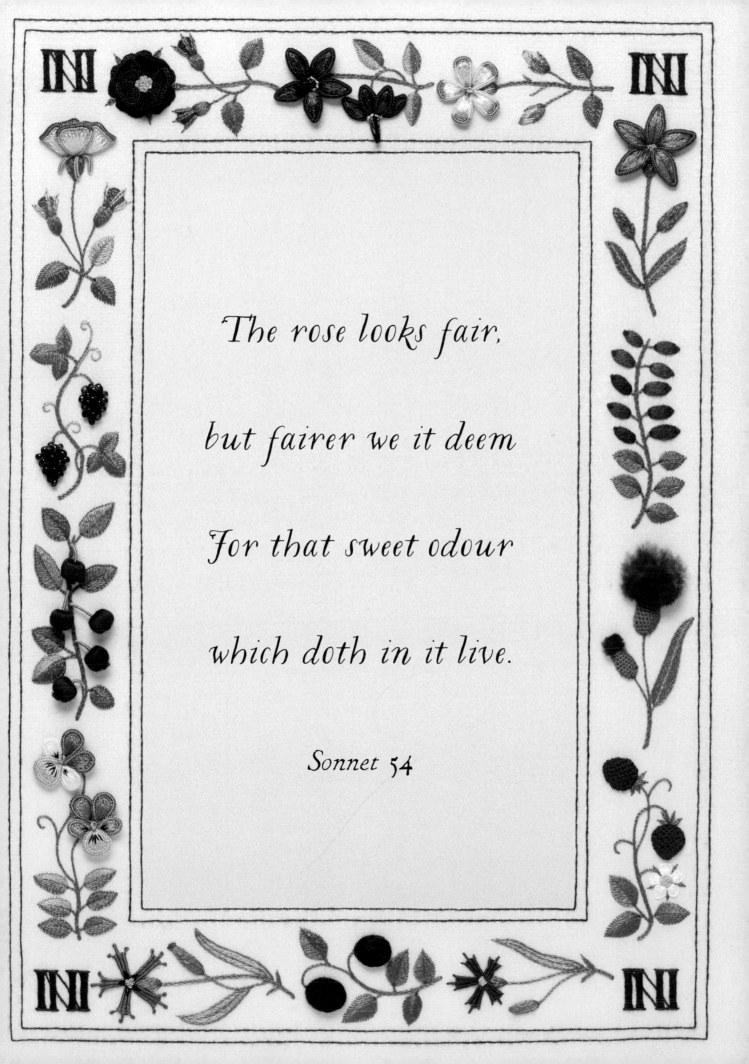

The rose looks fair,

but fairer we it deem

For that sweet odour

which doth in it live.

Sonnet 54

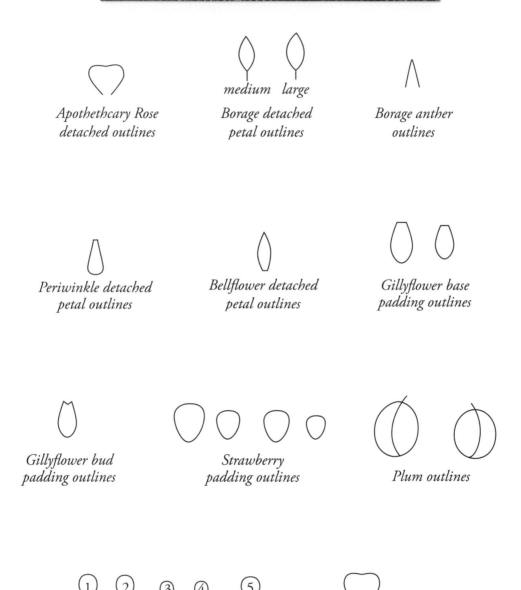

Apothethcary Rose
detached outlines

medium   large
Borage detached
petal outlines

Borage anther
outlines

Periwinkle detached
petal outlines

Bellflower detached
petal outlines

Gillyflower base
padding outlines

Gillyflower bud
padding outlines

Strawberry
padding outlines

Plum outlines

Heartsease detached
petal outlines

Sweet Briar detached
petal outlines

Diagrams are actual size

Apothecary Rose

Borage

Periwinkle

Sweet briar

Bellflower

Grapevine

Barberries

Redcurrants

Gillyflower

Heartsease

Strawberry

Cornflower

Plum

Knapweed

Before you begin...

The flowers in 'A Border of Shakespeare's Flowers' are worked with stumpwork and surface embroidery techniques. Before you begin, it will be helpful to familiarise yourself with the following information:

❋ Read through all the instructions before commencing work on the project. As a general rule, work all surface embroidery before applying any detached elements.

❋ The diagrams in the skeleton outline of the design, and the outlines for the detached elements, are actual size. The explanatory diagrams accompanying the instructions have often been enlarged for clarity.

❋ The skeleton outline provided for 'A Border of Shakespeare's Flowers' is the actual size that I embroidered—16.6 x 24 cm (6½ x 9½ in)—the same dimensions as the emailed image of Lady Anne Clifford's letter that inspired this piece. When visiting England in 2012, I was privileged to see the original—it was then that I realised that the actual letter was larger than I had imagined. As I found it quite a challenge to work at the smaller size, I recommend that you enlarge both the skeleton outline and the outlines for the detached elements by at least 10 per cent. (To see an image of the border of the original letter, go to the Skipton Castle website, www.skiptoncastle.co.uk, click on Fun Page on the left, then scroll down to Lady Anne Clifford—Writing Paper.)

❁ I have used the Au Ver à Soie stranded silk, Soie d'Alger, for most of the embroidery. Where possible, I have given DMC Stranded Cotton equivalents for the Soie d'Alger threads—the colours are close but not exactly the same. The embroidery is worked with one strand of thread, in a size 10 crewel needle, unless otherwise stipulated.

❁ It helps to cover all completed and unworked elements (except the one you are working on) with folded strips of white acid-free tissue paper, pinned to the sides of the frame, to prevent soiling and damage.

❁ For general information regarding techniques and equipment, please refer to the section 'Techniques, Equipment and Stitch Glossary'. If you are new to stumpwork, it is important that you read this section before undertaking any of the projects. As there is not the space here to provide detailed instructions on basic stumpwork techniques, you may like to refer to one of the stumpwork embroidery books listed in the Bibliography.

This is the complete list of requirements for this embroidery. For ease of use, the requirements of each individual element are repeated under its heading—for example, Cornflower requirements.

My original drawing of the design, and the outline which I used, measures 16.5 x 24 cm (6½ x 9½ in). The fabrics and frames suggested below are suitable for these dimensions. If you wish to enlarge the design outline, you will need to allow for this when selecting your fabrics and frame.

background fabric of choice
  (I used ivory silk satin): 32.5 x 40 cm (12½ x 15½ in); this measurement is suitable for a slate frame. If you are mounting the fabrics into a rectangular frame, you will need to allow extra around the edges for turnings
backing fabric (firm calico or muslin)
  sized to suit the slate or rectangular frame that you are using (at least 39 x 47 cm (16 x 19 in) to allow for hemmed edges if using a slate frame)

quilter's muslin: *seven 20 cm (8 in) squares*
grey felt: *5 x 8 cm (2 x 3 in)*
red felt: *5 x 8 cm (2 x 3 in)*
paper-backed fusible web:
  10 x 8 cm (4 x 3 in)
slate or rectangular frame of appropriate dimensions
  if using a slate frame, the top bars need a web length at least 36 cm (14½ in) and the spacer or stretcher bars need to be long enough to allow at least 44 cm (17½ in) between the top (web) bars.

10 or 13 cm (4 or 5 in) embroidery hoops
needles:
  crewel/embroidery sizes 5–10
  milliners/straw sizes 3–9
  sharps size 11 or 12
  tapestry sizes 26–28
  sharp yarn darners sizes 14–18
embroidery equipment (see page 244)

tracing paper
translucent removable adhesive tape: *19 mm (¾ in)*
Scotch Removable Magic Tape
thin card or manila folder
clear self-adhesive plastic (used for covering books):
  5 cm (2 in) squares
small amount of stuffing (fibre-fill) and a sate stick

fine silk tacking thread:
  YLI Silk Stitch #100 (col. 215)
machine sewing thread: *any colour*
ecru stranded thread: *DMC Ecru*

Stems & Leaves

dark olive stranded thread:
Soie d'Alger 2145 or DMC 469
medium olive stranded thread:
Soie d'Alger 3733 or DMC 471
dark green stranded thread:
Soie d'Alger 2134 or DMC 3346
medium green stranded thread:
Soie d'Alger 2133 or DMC 3347

Apothecary Rose

dark wine stranded thread:
Soie d'Alger 3046 or DMC 902
medium wine stranded thread:
Soie d'Alger 3045 or DMC 3802
medium yellow stranded thread:
Madeira Silk 113 or DMC 743

Barberries

medium orange stranded thread:
Soie d'Alger 645 or DMC 946
dark orange stranded thread:
Soie d'Alger 636 or DMC 900
russet stranded thread:
Soie d'Alger 2636 or DMC 919
rust stranded thread:
Soie d'Alger 2626 or DMC 400

Bellflower

dark mauve stranded thread:
Soie d'Alger 1314 or DMC 3834
medium mauve stranded thread:
Soie d'Alger 1313 or DMC 3835
dark yellow stranded thread:
Madeira Silk 114 or DMC 742

Borage

dark blue-violet stranded thread:
Soie d'Alger 4915 or DMC 791
medium blue-violet stranded thread:
Soie d'Alger 4914 or DMC 158
white stranded thread:
Soie d'Alger Blanc or DMC Blanc
black stranded thread:
Cifonda Art Silk Black or DMC 310
dark grey stranded thread:
Cifonda Art Silk 215 or DMC 317

Cornflower

medium blue stranded thread:
Soie d'Alger 4923 or DMC 798
dark blue stranded thread:
Soie d'Alger 1414 or DMC 796
old gold stranded thread:
Soie d'Alger 523 or DMC 733

Gillyflower

dark coral stranded thread:
Soie d'Alger 2916 or DMC 347
medium coral stranded thread:
Soie d'Alger 2915 or DMC 3328

Grapevine

dark grape stranded thread:
Soie d'Alger 4636 or DMC 902

OVERALL REQUIREMENTS (CONTINUED)

Heartsease

dark lavender stranded thread:
 Soie d'Alger 1343 or DMC 3746
medium lavender stranded thread:
 Soie d'Alger 1342 or DMC 340
dark yellow stranded thread:
 Madeira Silk 114 or DMC 742
light yellow stranded thread: *DMC 744*
orange stranded thread: *DMC 741*
dark purple fine silk thread:
 YLI Silk Stitch 50 col. 24

Knapweed

purple stranded thread:
 Soie d'Alger 1324 or DMC 3837
medium yellow stranded thread:
 Madeira Silk 113 or DMC 743

Periwinkle

light sky-blue stranded thread:
 Cifonda Art Silk 984 or DMC 162
medium sky-blue stranded thread:
 Cifonda Art Silk 987 or DMC 826
medium yellow stranded thread:
 Madeira Silk 113 or DMC 743

Plum

dark purple stranded thread:
 Soie d'Alger 3326 no match in DMC
dark plum stranded thread:
 Soie d'Alger 3316 no match in DMC
medium plum stranded thread:
 Soie d'Alger 5116 no match in DMC

Redcurrants

light red stranded thread:
 Soie d'Alger 944 or DMC 321
medium red stranded thread:
 Soie d'Alger 945 or DMC 498
dark red stranded thread:
 Soie d'Alger 946 or DMC 815
brown stranded thread: *DMC 898*

Strawberry

red twisted silk thread:
 Au Ver à Soie perlée 779
red stranded thread: *DMC 321*
white stranded thread:
 Soie d'Alger Blanc or DMC Blanc
medium yellow stranded thread:
 Madeira Silk 113 or DMC 743

Sweet Briar

dark rose stranded thread:
 Soie d'Alger 4634 or DMC 3726
medium rose stranded thread:
 Soie d'Alger 4633 or DMC 778
pale rose stranded thread:
 Soie d'Alger 4147 or DMC 225
old gold stranded thread:
 Soie d'Alger 523 or DMC 733

Initials & Border

variegated red stranded thread:
 Threadworx Hand Overdyed Floss col.1089 or
 Sampler Threads from The Gentle Art col. 0360
 (Cranberry) or DMC 4210

Mill Hill frosted glass beads 62056 (boysenberry)
Mill Hill frosted glass beads 60367 (garnet)
Mill Hill glass seed beads 00367 (garnet)
Mill Hill glass pebble beads 5025 (ruby)

---

33 gauge white covered wire (Sweet Briar detached petals): *three 9 cm (3½ in) lengths*

33 gauge white covered wire (Periwinkle detached petals): *five 9 cm (3½ in) lengths*

33 gauge white covered wire (Bellflower detached petals): *five 9 cm (3½ in) lengths (colour mauve if desired, Copic BV09 Violet)*

33 gauge white covered wire (Borage detached petals): *twelve 9 cm (3½ in) lengths (colour blue if desired, Copic BV08 Blue Violet)*

33 gauge white covered wire (Heartsease detached petals): *ten 9 cm (3½ in) lengths (if desired, colour four lengths violet for the upper petals, Copic BV08 Blue Violet; two lengths yellow for the lower petals, Copic Y15 Cadmium Yellow; and keep remaining four lengths of wire white for the paler side petals)*

33 gauge white covered wire (Apothecary Rose detached petals): *five 9 cm (3½ in) lengths (colour wine if desired, Copic R59 Cardinal)*

Drawn by Grace Christie, in
Needle and Thread *(1914)*

1. Mount the calico or muslin backing fabric and the background fabric of your choice into the square or rectangular frame (see page 238).

2. Using a fine lead pencil, trace the skeleton outlines of the design and border onto tracing paper. This will be the 'right side' of the tracing paper (it helps to write this on the tracing paper). Flip the tracing paper over and draw over the design outlines only on the back (not the border lines).

3. Position the 'right side' of the tracing paper against the muslin backing fabric (inside the back of the frame), checking that the border lines are aligned with the straight grain of the satin at the front. Temporarily secure the tracing paper with strips of masking tape. Using a stylus, draw over the border lines to transfer the outlines to the muslin backing.

4. With fine silk thread in a size 12 sharps needle, work a row of tacking/running stitches along both border lines. Make the stitches about 1 cm (½ in) long on the front (short on the back) and work a back stitch into each corner. These stitches, which will eventually be removed, are used when transferring the design to the front and also act as guide lines when working the red back stitch lines for the border.

5. With the tracing paper right side up, position the tracing over the satin, lining up the traced border lines with the tacked border lines. Temporarily secure the edges of the tracing paper to the satin with strips of masking tape. Using a stylus, draw over the design lines to transfer the skeleton outline of the design to the satin (it is essential to have a board or book underneath the frame of fabric to provide a firm surface).

6. Embroider each flower following the individual instructions. The flowers are listed in alphabetical order, however, it would be easier to work from the top left corner to the bottom right corner if you are right-handed, or from the top right corner to the bottom left corner if you are left-handed.

7. Work the initials and border lines when all the flowers have been completed.

STEMS & LEAVES

All the stems, and some of the leaves, are worked in stem stitch (see page 262). Most of the leaves are embroidered in either buttonhole stitch or fishbone stitch. The diagrams for the working of these leaves are included here in case you choose to work all of the stems and leaves before commencing on the flowers.

To Work Leaves in Buttonhole Stitch

The leaves are worked with one strand of green thread in a size 10 crewel needle. Starting at the base of the leaf, embroider one side with long buttonhole stitches, worked at an angle—the ridge of the buttonhole forms the leaf outline. Using the same or a contrasting green thread, embroider the remaining side of the leaf with long buttonhole stitches, inserting the needle into the base of the buttonhole stitches of the other side to avoid a gap in the centre of the leaf. The slanted buttonhole stitches may be started at the tip of the leaf and worked towards the base, if preferred.

To Work Leaves in Fishbone Stitch

The leaves are worked with one strand of green thread in a size 10 crewel needle. Starting at the tip, work the leaf with close fishbone stitches, making sure the stitches start just outside the traced outline.

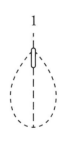

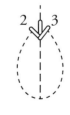

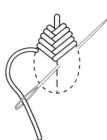

APOTHECARY Rose

*What's in a name? That which we call a rose
By any other name would smell as sweet.*

Romeo & Juliet (ii.2)

Roses have been revered for thousands of years, both for their fragrant beauty and their cosmetic and therapeutic properties—the Chinese, the Greeks and the Romans were all passionate about them. The Apothecary Rose, *Rosa gallica officinalis,* also known as the French or Gallic Rose, the Rose of Provins and the Red Rose of Lancaster, is a bushy small shrub with dull green foliage and fragrant, crimson flowers which open wide to reveal golden stamens. The flowers are followed by deep red hips in the autumn. The Apothecary Rose has been grown for centuries for its medicinal qualities (both 'Apothecary' and *officinalis* refer to its use as a legitimate medicinal herb, listed in the pharmacopeias of many countries). In his sixteenth-century herbal, Gerard discusses the 'vertues' of roses at length:

*Rose embroidery motif
(John Overton)*

The distilled water of Roses is good for the strengthening of the heart, and refreshing of the spirits, and likewise for all things that require a gentle cooling. The same being put in junketing dishes, cakes, sauces, and many other pleasant things, giveth a fine and delectable taste. It mitigateth the paine of the eies proceeding of a hot cause, bringeth sleep, which also the fresh roses themselves provoke through their sweet and pleasant smell.

  John Gerard, THE HERBALL (1597)

Rosewater, distilled from rose petals by apothecaries, was much favoured for bathing the face and hands, a practice which would have been familiar to Shakespeare:

Let one attend him with a silver basin
Full of rose-water and bestrew'd with flowers.

  THE TAMING OF THE SHREW (Introduction, 1)

There are more than seventy references to the rose in Shakespeare's plays and sonnets, in many cases as an emblem of all that is fair and lovely, although he was very much aware of the flower's fleeting life:

The Rose looks fair, but fairer we it deem
For that sweet odour that doth in it live.
The canker-blooms have full as deep a dye
As the perfumed tincture of the Roses,
Hang on such thorns, and play as wantonly
When summer's breath their masked buds discloses;
But, for their virtue only is their show,
They live unwoo'd and unrespected fade;
Die to themselves. Sweet Roses do not so;
Of their sweet deaths are sweetest odours made.

  SONNET 54

The reference to a rose in Romeo and Juliet—where Juliet argues that the 'names' of things do not matter, only what things 'are'—encapsulates the central struggle and tragedy of the play. It is one of the most famous quotations from Shakespeare.

Painted engraving of a Rosa gallica by Pierre-Joseph Redouté (1759–1840).

Requirements

dark wine stranded thread:
Soie d'Alger 3046 or DMC 902

medium wine stranded thread:
Soie d'Alger 3045 or DMC 3802

medium yellow stranded thread:
Madeira Silk 113 or DMC 743

dark olive stranded thread:
Soie d'Alger 2145 or DMC 469

dark green stranded thread:
Soie d'Alger 2134 or DMC 3346

quilter's muslin: *20 cm (8 in) square*

tracing paper: *1.5 cm squares*

clear self-adhesive plastic (used for covering books):
5 cm squares
machine sewing thread: *any colour that contrasts
with the wine colour*

33 gauge white covered wire (detached petals):
*five 9 cm (3½ in) lengths (colour wine if desired,
Copic R59 Cardinal)*

*actual size
in border*

Stems

The stems are worked in stem stitch with one strand of thread in a size 10 crewel needle.

1. Using dark olive thread, work a row of stem stitch along the bud stem lines.

2. Starting at the base with dark olive thread, work a row of stem stitch along the main stem line.

3. Starting at the base with dark green thread, work a second row of stem stitch on the left side of the first row.

Leaves

The leaves are embroidered in fishbone stitch with one strand of dark olive thread.

1. Starting at the tip, work the leaf with close fishbone stitches, making sure the stitches start just outside the traced outline.

2. Work the leaf stalks in stem stitch.

*completed
stems & leaves*

Rose Bud

1. Using medium wine thread, work the bud petals with long buttonhole stitches, the ridge of the stitch forming the top edge of the petals.

2. Using dark olive thread, outline the bud base with small back stitches. Work three chain stitches, inside the outline, to pad the base. Embroider the base in satin stitch, working from the stem end into the base of the petals and enclosing the outline.

3. The sepals are worked with detached chain stitches using one strand of dark olive thread. Work three chain stitches from the top of the base over the petals. Make the tie-down stitch slightly elongated to give a pointed end to the sepal.

completed bud

Rose

BACKGROUND PETALS

The background petals are worked with one strand of dark wine thread.

Work a row of long and short buttonhole stitch along the outer edge of the petals, working the stitches close together and keeping the stitch direction towards the centre of the rose (this row of stitching will come at least halfway down the petal). Fill the petals with long and short stitch, leaving the centre of the rose unstitched.

SEPALS

Using one strand of dark olive thread, work two chain stitches, one inside the other, at the junction of the petals to form the sepals. Make the smaller chain stitch first then the second stitch around it (work this with a long 'tie down' stitch to give a point the end of the sepal).

DETACHED PETALS

The detached petals are embroidered in detached buttonhole stitch (see Stitch Guide) worked within a framework of wire. The shaped wire is attached temporarily to a template mounted on a hoop of fabric to facilitate the working.

1. Mount a piece of muslin into a 10 cm (4 in) hoop (drum tight). Trace a detached petal outline onto a small square of tracing paper and attach this to the centre of the hoop of fabric with a larger square of self-adhesive plastic.

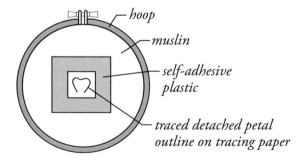

hoop

muslin

self-adhesive plastic

traced detached petal outline on tracing paper

This will be the template on which to work the detached buttonhole petals (it can be used for each of the five petals but as it tends to get damaged with use it may be easier to renew it for the third or fourth petal).

2. Using machine thread in a crewel needle, couch a piece of wire around the petal outline (six couching stitches), shaping as you go with tweezers, and leaving two tails of wire of similar length at each end. These couching stitches go through the plastic-covered muslin (these are the only stitches that do go through the background fabric—the stitches to work the petal are detached). Temporarily hold the tails of wire to the muslin with masking tape.

3. Using one long strand of dark wine thread in a size 28 tapestry needle, knot the thread to the wire at the lower left corner of the petal outline (leaving a 5 cm/2 in tail of thread), then work a row of detached buttonhole stitch around the inside of the wire (approximately 25 stitches, a thread width apart). Do not pull the stitches too tight as the next row of detached buttonhole stitch needs to be worked into them. Knot the thread to the wire at the lower right hand corner of the petal, then take the thread across the base of the petal to the lower left corner, ready to start the next row of detached buttonhole stitch.

4. Continue working rows of buttonhole stitch in the same direction (decreasing where necessary by missing a space in the previous row), until the shape is nearly filled (about four rows), stopping with the thread at the centre of the petal. Work this thread to the base of the petal, closing any gap as you go.

5. Slide the needle and thread to the lower right corner of the petal, then work a row of detached buttonhole stitch around the outside edge of the petal to form a ruffled edge, taking the needle into the spaces between the buttonhole stitches in the first row. Leave another tail of thread (do not trim).

6. Cut the couching threads from the back of the hoop and carefully remove the petal. Make another four petals—two more with dark wine thread and two with medium wine thread. Renew the plastic-covered template when necessary.

Apply Detached Petals

Using a fine lead pencil, mark five equally spaced dots around the edge of the rose centre (offset them so that they are halfway between the embroidered petals if desired). The wire tails for each petal will be inserted through two adjoining dots, using a yarn darner to make the hole. Apply the petals one at a time, bending the wire tails behind the embroidered petals and securing to the back temporarily with masking tape (the wires for each petal are separated but do share a common hole with neighbouring petals). Secure the wires with tiny stitches. Do not trim the wire tails until the rose centre has been worked.

Rose Centre

Using two strands of medium yellow thread in a size 8 milliners needle, work French knots (one wrap) to fill the centre of the rose. Shape the detached petals with tweezers, then trim the wire tails at the back.

completed rose

*actual size
in sampler*

36

Borage

Borage is a plant of the Mediterranean but has been cultivated in Britain for many centuries. Also known as Starflower, Borage (*Borago officinalis*) is an annual herb with pretty blue, pink or white star-shaped flowers with distinct black centres. Along with fennel, thyme, parsley, mint and chives, borage was a commonly cultivated culinary plant in medieval gardens. With its fresh, cucumber-like flavour, it was often used in salads or as a garnish. *Borago officinalis* was also credited with lightening the heart, as well as the taste buds (the Latin species name *officinalis* was reserved for vital medicines), and is still used in fruit cup syrups such as Pimm's. Whether it has any intoxicating properties is now considered doubtful, but certainly it was once used with this intention:

Those of our time do use the floures in sallads, to exhilerate and make the minde glad. There be also many things made of them, used for the comfort of the heart, to drive away sorrow, & increase the joy of the minde. The leaves and floures of Borrage put into wine make men and women glad and merry, driving away all sadnesse, dulnesse, and melancholy.

John Gerard, THE HERBALL (1597)

Mentioned in Shakespeare's plays as a herb 'for courage', a Borage flower was said to be floated on the stirrup cups of knights departing for the Crusades to give them courage. Borage was also a popular motif in sixteenth- and seventeenth-century needlework.

Borage designs: above; slip for a cushion (c1600), below; transfer pattern in **The Embroidress** *(1930s)*

Requirements

dark blue-violet stranded thread:
Soie d'Alger 4915 or DMC 791

medium blue-violet stranded thread:
Soie d'Alger 4914 or DMC 158

white stranded thread:
Soie d'Alger Blanc or DMC Blanc

black stranded thread:
Cifonda Art Silk Black or DMC 310

dark grey stranded thread:
Cifonda Art Silk 215 or DMC 317

dark green stranded thread:
Soie d'Alger 2134 or DMC 3346

medium green stranded thread:
Soie d'Alger 2133 or DMC 3347

dark olive stranded thread:
Soie d'Alger 2145 or DMC 469

quilter's muslin: *20 cm (8 in) square in a
10 or 13 cm (4 or 5 in) hoop*

33 gauge white covered wire (detached petals):
*twelve 9 cm (3½ in) lengths (colour blue if desired,
Copic BV08 Blue Violet)*

*actual size
in border*

Stems

The stems are worked in stem stitch with one strand of thread in a size 10 crewel needle.

1. Using dark green thread, work a row of stem stitch along the side flower stem line.

2. Starting at the base with dark olive thread, work a row of stem stitch along the main stem line. Using dark green thread, work a second row of stem stitch on the left side of the first row.

Leaves

The leaves are embroidered in buttonhole stitch with one strand of thread.

1. Using dark green thread, embroider the lower side of each leaf with long buttonhole stitches, worked at an angle (the ridge of the buttonhole forms the leaf outline). Using medium green thread, embroider the upper side of each leaf with long buttonhole stitches, inserting the needle into the base of the buttonhole stitches of the lower side to avoid a gap in the centre of the leaf.

2. Work the leaf stems in stem stitch with dark green thread.

Borage Flowers

The detached petals and anthers may be worked on the same hoop of fabric.

DETACHED PETALS

Nine detached petals are required—five large and four medium. They are all worked the same way.

1. Mount muslin into a small hoop and trace nine petal outlines (five large and four medium) and two anther outlines (the petals and anthers may be worked on two hoops of fabric if preferred).

completed stems
& leaves

2. Using one strand of dark blue-violet thread in a size 10 crewel needle, couch a piece of wire around a petal outline (six couching stitches), shaping as you go with tweezers, and leaving two tails of wire at the base that touch but do not cross. Buttonhole-stitch the wire to the muslin. Park the thread at the side to use later.

3. Using medium blue-violet thread, embroider the lower half of the petal in long and short stitch, working from the base of the petal towards the point. Park the thread to use later. Work the top half of the petal with dark blue-violet thread, blending the stitches into the medium blue-violet.

4. With one strand of medium blue-violet thread, work a row of split stitch to form a centre line in the petal. Work all petals the same way. Carefully cut out the petals—the five larger petals for the upper flower and the four smaller petals for the side flower.

Detached Anthers

Two detached anthers are required—both the same size and worked the same way. A 9 cm (3½ in) length and a 4.5 cm (1¾ in) length of wire are required for each anther. The anthers are worked with one strand of thread in a size 12 sharps needle.

1. Mount muslin into a small hoop and trace two anther outlines (the anthers may be worked with the detached petals).

2. Bend a 9 cm (3½ in) length of wire in half to form a sharp V. Using black thread, couch the wire around the anther outline, working one stitch at the point and a stitch 7 mm (5/8 in) down from the point on each side. Stitch the wire to the muslin with overcast stitch.

3. Place a 4.5 cm (1¾ in) length of wire inside the bent wire to form the centre of the anther (one end inside the stitched point of the wire). With black

7 mm

40

thread, couch, then overcast the wire to the muslin, working the stitches as close to the point as possible.

4. Using one strand of dark grey thread, embroider each side of the anther, between the wires, with long and short stitch.

5. Cut out the shape (close to the stitching at the lower edge), avoiding the tails of wire. Carefully bend the centre wire behind the anther and trim to 2 mm. Using tweezers, squeeze the sides of the anther towards each other (enclosing the trimmed centre tail) to form a cone shape.

To Complete the Upper Flower

The upper flower has five detached petals and an anther.

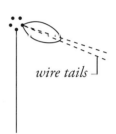

wire tails

1. Draw a circle of five dots (the wire insertion points), very close together, at the end of the main stem. Insert the wire tails of the detached petals through five individual holes (as close to each other as possible), using a large yarn darner. Bend the wire tails under each petal and secure with small stitches (using white thread). Do not cut the wire tails until the flower is finished.

2. Using a yarn darner, insert the anther wires through one hole in the centre of the flower. Secure the wire tails behind the stem (check that the gap in the anther cone is at the back).

3. Using tweezers, adjust the shape and position of the petals and anther before working French knots to form the tubercles at the base of the petals. Using one strand of white thread in a size 9 milliners needle, work French knots (one wrap loosely worked), between the petals and the anthers to form a white 'circle' at the base of the anther. Adjust the position of the petals and anther if necessary then trim the wires at the back.

completed upper flower

To Complete the Side Flower

The side flower has four detached petals and an anther.

1. Draw a semicircle of four dots (the wire insertion points), very close together, at the end of the side flower stem. The wire tails of the detached petals are inserted through these four individual holes (as close to each other as possible), using a yarn darner. Apply the side petals first, then the two centre petals. Bend the wire tails under each petal and secure with small stitches. Do not cut the wire tails until the flower is finished.

2. Using a yarn darner, insert the anther wires through one hole at the base of the detached petals and secure the tails of wire behind the stem (check that the gap in the anther is at the back).

3. Using tweezers, adjust the shape and position of the petals and anther before working French knots to form the tubercles at the base of the petals. Using one strand of white thread in a size 9 milliners needle, work French knots (one wrap loosely worked), between the petals and the anthers to form a white 'semicircle' at the base of the anther. Adjust the position of the petals and anther if necessary, then trim the wires at the back.

completed side flower

actual size in sampler

42

Periwinkle

Chaucer's 'fresh pervinke [periwinkle], rich of hue', *Vinca minor*, an essential constituent of any respectable flowery mead, has a long history. The name *Vinca* originates from the Latin *vincio*, 'to bind', alluding to the long spreading stems which were frequently used to make wreaths and love knots, allegorically binding lovers together. In his seventeenth-century *Complete Herbal and English Physician*, Nicholas Culpeper maintained that 'the leaves of periwinkle eaten by man and wife together, will cause love between them.' However, in the Middle Ages the flower was also a symbol of death and immortality. Criminals wore a garland of periwinkle at their execution and it was known in Italy as Death's Flower—*fiore di morte*.

Periwinkle is also a colour in the blue and purple family, its name being derived from the 'lavender blue' of the periwinkle. The first recorded use of periwinkle as a colour name in English was in 1895. It is possible that periwinkle flowers were the origin of 'something blue' for the bride to wear. The periwinkle was also regarded as a valuable medicinal plant and was used as a remedy for various ailments, including high blood pressure, and as a gargle to cure a sore throat.

Requirements

light sky-blue stranded thread:
Cifonda Art Silk 984 or DMC 162

medium sky-blue stranded thread:
Cifonda Art Silk 987 or DMC 826

medium yellow stranded thread:
Madeira Silk 113 or DMC 743

ecru stranded thread:
DMC Ecru

dark green stranded thread:
Soie d'Alger 2134 or DMC 3346

dark olive stranded thread:
Soie d'Alger 2145 or DMC 469

quilter's muslin: *20 cm (8 in) square in a
10 or 13 cm (4 or 5 in) hoop*

33 gauge white covered wire (detached petals):
five 9 cm (3½ in) lengths

*actual size
in border*

Stems

The stems are worked in stem stitch with one strand of thread in a size 10 crewel needle.

1. Starting at the base with dark olive thread, work a row of stem stitch along the main stem line. Using dark green thread, work a second row of stem stitch on the left of the first row.

2. Using dark green thread, work a row of stem stitch along all the side stem lines.

Leaves

The leaves are embroidered in buttonhole stitch with one strand of thread.

1. Using dark olive thread, embroider the lower side of the leaves with long buttonhole stitches, worked at an angle (the ridge of the buttonhole forms the leaf outline). Using dark green thread, embroider the upper side of the leaves with long buttonhole stitches, inserting the needle into the base of the buttonhole stitches of the lower side to avoid a gap in the centre of the leaf.

2. Work the leaf stems in stem stitch with dark green thread.

*completed
stems & leaves*

Periwinkle Bud

The flower bud is worked with one strand of thread.

1. Using medium sky-blue thread, outline the bud with small back stitches. Work three long chain stitches inside the outline to pad the bud. Embroider the bud in satin stitch, enclosing the outline.

2. Using one strand of dark green thread and starting at the stem end, work three chain stitches over the lower half of the embroidered bud to form the sepals.

completed bud

Periwinkle Flower

BASE

The flower base is worked with one strand of medium sky-blue thread.

1. Outline the base with small back stitches, leaving a small gap at the top of the base. Work three or four long chain stitches, inside the outline, to pad the base.

2. Embroider the base in satin stitch, enclosing the outline.

DETACHED PETALS

1. Mount muslin into a small hoop and trace five petal outlines.

2. Using one strand of light sky-blue thread, couch a length of wire around the petal outline, working two couching stitches on both sides of the petal but no stitches across the top edge, as this will be worked in medium sky-blue (there is a tiny gap between the wire tails at the base of the petal). Starting with light sky-blue thread, buttonhole-stitch the wire to the muslin along one side of the petal, stopping just before the upper corner is reached. Park the thread and change to medium sky-blue to work the top edge of the petal. Return to the light sky-blue thread to buttonhole the remaining side of the petal.

3. Work a row of long and short buttonhole stitch inside the wire at the top edge of the petal with medium sky-blue thread. Using light sky-blue thread, embroider the remainder of the petal in long and short stitch, blending into the medium sky-blue edge. Carefully cut out the petals.

completed petal

To Complete the Periwinkle Flower

1. Draw a circle of five dots (the wire insertion points), very close together, at the top edge of the flower base. Insert the wire tails of the detached petals through five individual holes (as close to each other as possible), using a large yarn darner. Bend the wire tails under each petal and secure with small stitches using ecru thread. Do not cut the wire tails until the flower is finished.

2. Using tweezers, adjust the shape and position of the petals. With one strand of medium sky-blue thread in a size 12 sharps needle, work a chain stitch into the base of each petal, coming out at the wire insertion point and taking the needle carefully through the petal to the back of the work (do not pull the thread too tight as it may flatten the petal).

completed flower

3. Using two strands of medium yellow thread in a milliners needle, work a loose French knot (one wrap) to form the centre of the flower (if your tension is tight you may need to use three strands of thread). Trim the wires.

*actual size
in sampler*

Bellflower

The spreading Bellflower, *Campanula patula*, with its delicate white, violet-blue or violet-pink flowers, inhabits meadows, open woodland, hedgerows and waste land. With its characteristic bell-shaped flowers, the genus *Campanula* takes its name from the Latin for 'little bell'. Pilgrims carried bells to announce their presence along narrow country byways, and in Italian herbals bellflowers were named *herba San Cristoforo* after the patron saint of travellers. On arrival at the shrine of Saint Christopher, pilgrims bought badges, often in the form of a pilgrim's handbell, which they wore as souvenirs and tokens of blessing.

White, blue, pink or purple bellflowers, along with pinks, snowdrops, marguerites, helichrysum and meadowsweet, were the flowers likely to be chosen to make the wreaths, crowns and garlands that were an essential component of the many religious festivals in the medieval calendar.

BELLFLOWER : METHOD

Requirements

dark mauve stranded thread:
Soie d'Alger 1314 or DMC 3834

medium mauve stranded thread:
Soie d'Alger 1313 or DMC 3835

dark yellow stranded thread:
Madeira Silk 114 or DMC 742

medium olive stranded thread:
Soie d'Alger 3733 or DMC 471

dark olive stranded thread:
Soie d'Alger 2145 or DMC 469

ecru stranded thread: *DMC Ecru*

quilter's muslin: *20 cm (8 in) square in a
10 or 13 cm (4 or 5 in) hoop*

33 gauge white covered wire (detached petals):
*five 9 cm (3½ in) lengths (colour mauve if desired,
Copic BV09 Violet)*

*actual size
in border*

Stems

The stems are worked in stem stitch with one strand of dark olive thread in a size 10 crewel needle.

1. Starting at the base, work a row of stem stitch along the main stem line. Work a second row of stem stitch on the left side of the first row.

2. Starting at the main stem, work a row of stem stitch along the bud stem lines.

Leaves

The leaves are embroidered in stem and split stitch with one strand of thread.

1. Using dark olive thread, outline the leaf in stem stitch.

2. With medium olive thread, work the central vein in split stitch.

3. Using dark olive thread, fill the space between the central vein and the outline with rows of split stitch.

Bellflower Buds

The flower bud is worked with one strand of thread.

1. Using dark mauve thread, outline the bud with small back stitches. Work straight stitches inside the outline to pad the bud. Embroider the bud in satin stitch, enclosing the outline.

2. Using one strand of dark olive thread and starting at the stem end, work three chain stitches over the lower half of the embroidered bud to form the sepals.

Bellflower

BASE

The flower base is worked with one strand of dark mauve thread.

1. Outline the base with small back stitches, leaving a small gap at the top of the base. Work three or four long chain stitches, inside the outline, to pad the base.

completed bud

2. Embroider the base in satin stitch, enclosing the outline.

Detached Petals

1. Mount muslin into a small hoop and trace five petal outlines.

2. Using one strand of dark mauve thread, couch a piece of wire around a petal outline, shaping as you go with tweezers, and leaving two tails of wi the base that touch but do not cross. Buttonhole-stitch the wire to the mu Park the thread at the side to use later.

3. Using medium mauve thread, embroider the petal in long and short sti working from the base of the petal towards the point.

4. With dark mauve thread, work a row of split stitch to form a centre line in the petal. Work all petals the same way. Carefully cut out the petals.

completed flower

To Complete the Bellflower

1. Draw a circle of five dots (the wire insertion points), very close together, at the top edge of the flower base. Insert the wire tails of the detached petals through five individual holes (as close to each other as possible), using a large yarn darner. Bend the wire tails under each petal and secure with small stitches using ecru thread. Do not cut the wire tails until the flower is finished.

2. Adjust the shape and position of the petals with tweezers.

3. Using one strand of dark yellow thread in a milliners needle, work five French knots (one wrap) to form the centre of the flower. Trim the wires.

Barberry

The Barberry, *Berberis vulgaris*, was a favourite perennial shrub in Victorian borders, as it was an eyecatching plant in two seasons—in spring, its small bright yellow flowers hung in grape-like clusters along the stem, while in autumn it displayed bright reddish orange oval berries. The green foliage, with its accompanying blue or yellow tinge, was also admired. It is believed that the name comes from the Arabic word, *berberis*, meaning 'a shell', as the glossy leaves are like the inside of an oyster shell.

Barberry
embroidery motifs

The Barberry was also cultivated for its sharply acidic fruit, which could be pickled and used for a garnish, or boiled with sugar to make a refreshing jelly. The leaves could be added to salads or made into a sauce, as described by Gerard:

The leaves are used of divers to season meate with, and in stead of a sallad, as be those of Sorrell ... The grean leaves of the Barbery bush stamped, and made into sauce, as that made of Sorrell, called greene sauce, doth coole hot stomackes, and those that are vexed with hot burning agues, and procureth appetite. The conserve made of the fruite and sugar performeth all those things before remembred, but with better force and successe.

John Gerard, *The Herball* (1597)

The Barberry was also known as the Jaundice Tree, as an infusion of its yellow inner bark was said to cure jaundice. It possesses powerful antibiotic properties which have been proved effective against several infectious diseases, including cholera. A fine yellow dye extracted from the distinctive yellow root-bark was widely used to dye wool, linen and

BARBERRY : METHOD

Requirements

medium orange stranded thread:
Soie d'Alger 645 or DMC 946

dark orange stranded thread:
Soie d'Alger 636 or DMC 900

russet stranded thread:
Soie d'Alger 2636 or DMC 919

rust stranded thread:
Soie d'A lger 2626 or DMC 400

dark olive stranded thread:
Soie d'Alger 2145 or DMC 469

*actual size
in border*

leather.

Stems

The stems are worked in stem stitch with one strand of dark olive thread in a size 10 crewel needle.

Starting at the base, work a row of stem stitch along the main stem line.

Work a second row of stem stitch on the left side of the first row.

Leaves

The leaves are embroidered in fishbone stitch with one strand of dark olive thread.

1. Starting at the tip, work the leaf with close fishbone stitches, making sure the stitches start just outside the traced outline.

*completed
stems & leaves*

2. Work the leaf stalks in stem stitch.

Barberries

The barberries are worked in satin stitch with one strand of thread. Work four berries with russet thread, three berries with dark orange and three with medium orange.

1. Outline the berry in back stitch. Work straight stitches inside the outline to pad the shape.

2. Embroider the berry in satin stitch, enclosing the outline and working the stitches towards the tip of the berry.

3. With two strands of rust thread in a size 9 milliners needle, work a Fro knot (one wrap) at the end of each berry.

4. Work the berry stalks in stem stitch with one strand of dark olive thre

completed barberries

actual size
in sampler

Gillyflower

Sir, the year growing ancient,
Not yet on summer's death, nor on the birth
Of trembling winter, the fairest
flowers o' the season
Are our carnation, and streak'd gillyvors,

The Winter's Tale (iv.4)

a Carnation

The Carnation, *Dianthus caryophyllus*, was also known as the Gillyflower (Gillofloure) in the seventeenth century, when there were at least 360 named varieties. The species name comes from the Latin *caryophyllus*, which means 'cloves' (the Gillyflower was sometimes known as the Clove-Gillofloure because of its rich, pungent smell). Together with Pinks, Sweet Williams and Picotees, Carnations belong to the *Dianthus* genus of plants and have been cultivated for at least 2000 years.

Carnation embroidery motif (John Overton)

The emblem of love and affection, the sweetly scented flowers of the Carnation were originally a bright pinkish purple colour, giving it its name—'carnation' was a colour (pale red or deep blush) in the sixteenth century, as well as a flower. It was originally spelled 'coronation', which reflects its early use in garlands, wreaths and crowns.

Gillyflower
embroidery motif
(Richard Shorleyker)

Carnations added a spicy clove flavour to ales and wines and were popularly called 'sops in wine' by Elizabethan bon vivants.

Bring hether the Pincke and purple Cullambine,
With Gelliflowers;
Bring Coronations, and Sops-in-wine
Worne of Paramoures:
Strowe me the ground with Daffadowndillies,
And Cowslips, and Kingcups, and loved Lillies:
    Edmund Spenser (1552–99), 'A DITTY'

When he wrote *The Winter's Tale*, Shakespeare had left London and returned to his home and garden in Stratford, where he was to end his days. In his writing, he often associated the seasons of the year with the lives of men and women—from the 'springtime' of childhood to the 'trembling winter' of old age. In the quotation from the play on the opposite page, Perdita is talking about midsummer—middle age—and the flowers—carnations and gillyvors—which bloom in gardens at that time (*streak'd gillyvors* were a variegated form of carnation developed by gardeners).

Requirements

dark coral stranded thread:
Soie d'Alger 2916 or DMC 347

medium coral stranded thread:
Soie d'Alger 2915 or DMC 3328

dark green stranded thread:
Soie d'Alger 2134 or DMC 3346

medium green stranded thread:
Soie d'Alger 2133 or DMC 3347

grey felt and paper-backed fusible web:
5 x 8 cm (3 x 2 in)

eyebrow comb

*actual size
in border*

Stems

The stems are worked in stem stitch with one strand of dark green thread in a size 10 crewel needle.

1. Starting at the base, work a row of stem stitch along the main flower stem line.

2. Starting at the base, work a row of stem stitch next to the previous row then veer to the left along the bud stem line.

Leaves

The leaves are embroidered in stem and split stitch with one strand of thread.

1. Using dark green thread, outline the leaf in stem stitch.

2. Work the central vein in split stitch with medium green thread.

3. Using dark green thread, embroider the leaf with rows of stem stitch.

Gillyflower

BASE

1. Trace two gillyflower base padding shapes, one the actual size and one slightly smaller, and one gillyflower bud padding shape, onto paper-backed fusible web then fuse to the grey felt. Carefully cut out the shapes.

2. With one strand of dark green thread in a size 10 crewel needle, apply the flower base padding shapes to the background fabric with small stab stitches, applying the smallest shape first (apply the padding with the fusible web side uppermost—this will help prevent the felt fibres from working their way through the covering of detached buttonhole stitch).

completed stem & leaf

3. Work a row of buttonhole stitch around the curved outside edge of the base (stitches about 1.5 mm apart) to outline the shape.

4. Starting at the top straight edge of the base, enclose the padding (and buttonhole outline) with rows of corded detached buttonhole stitch, using one strand of dark green thread in a size 28 tapestry needle. The laid threads (cord) are worked from left to right, as are the detached buttonhole stitches, as shown in the diagram. Increase or decrease stitches at the beginning and end of rows as required (work 4–5 detached buttonhole stitches in the first row, increasing to 6 or 7). A sliver of card inserted temporarily between the stitches and the felt may facilitate the working of this covering (this is optional).

1 *straight stitch (cord)*
2 *detached buttonhole*
3 *straight stitch (cord)*
4 *detached buttonhole over cord*
5 *straight stitch (cord) (and so on....)*

Petals

The gillyflower petals are worked with close rows of Turkey knots, using two strands of thread in a size 8 or 9 milliners needle.

completed flower

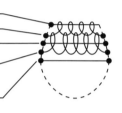

1. Starting at the top edge of the base, work a row of 5–6 Turkey knots with two strands of dark coral thread. Work successive rows of Turkey knots, above this first row (within the side lines) as follows:

- work 4 more rows with two strands of dark coral thread
- work 3–4 rows using one strand each of dark and medium coral thread
- work 3–4 rows with two strands of medium coral thread

2. Using sharp scissors and an eyebrow comb, cut and comb the Turkey knots to achieve the desired effect.

Gillyflower Bud

BASE

1. Trace a bud base padding shape on to paper-backed fusible web then fuse to the grey felt. Carefully cut out the shape.

2. With one strand of dark green thread, apply the felt shape (web side up) to the background fabric with small stab stitches, then work a row of detached buttonhole stitch around the curved outside edge of the base.

3. Starting at the top edge of the base, enclose the padding with rows of corded detached buttonhole stitch, as for the gillyflower.

PETALS

The gillyflower bud petals are worked with Turkey knots, using two strands of dark coral thread, as follows:

- work 2 Turkey knots at the top of the base
- work the row above with three Turkey knots
- work two knots in the next row then the final row with one Turkey knot

Cut and comb the Turkey knots to achieve the desired effect.

completed bud

*actual size
in sampler*

Strawberry

Have you not sometimes seen a handkerchief
Spotted with strawberries in your wife's hand?

Othello (iii.3)

Strawberry
embroidery
motifs (Richard
Shorleyker)

The much-loved Strawberry, *Fragaria vesca,* known also as the wild strawberry, woodland strawberry or Alpine strawberry, is a perennial plant that has been consumed by humans since the Stone Age. The woodland strawberry was first cultivated in ancient Persia, where farmers knew it as *toot farangi.* Its seeds were later taken along the Silk Road towards Europe where it was widely cultivated until the eighteenth century, when it began to be replaced by the garden strawberry (a hybrid that goes under the name *Fragaria* x *ananassa*). The Old English name, *streawberige,* derives not from the plants being mulched with straw, as is commonly thought, but more likely from the runners 'strewing' fresh plants in all directions. Thomas Tusser, prolific sixteenth-century poet and also farmer, wrote:

Wife unto thy garden and set me a plot
With strawberry rootes of the best to be got;
Such growing abroade among thornes in the wood
Well chosen and picked proove excellent good.
  Thomas Tusser, 'September', Five Hundred Points
of Good Husbandry (1557)

The wild strawberry was gathered from hedgerows and woodlands and was renowned for its luscious taste. The strawberry leaves and berries were used medicinally to cool inflamed wounds and gums, and to clear the face of spots. According to Gerard:

The leaves boyled and applied in manner of a pultis taketh away the burning heate in wounds: the decoction thereof strengthneth the gummes, and fastneth the teeth. The distilled water drunke with white Wine is good against the passion of the heart, reviving the spirits, and making the heart merry. The ripe Straw-berries quench thirst, and take away, if they be often used, the rednesse and heate of the face'

John Gerard, THE HERBALL (1597)

The strawberry's decorative habit of fruiting and flowering at the same time has also made it a very popular subject with embroiderers and illuminators through the ages.

Shakespeare's mention of the strawberry and the nettle in *Henry V* refers to the belief in his day that companion planting affected plants to such an extent that they absorbed each other's 'virtues and faults'. Thus, sweet flowers were planted near fruit trees, with the idea of improving the flavour of the fruit, and foul-smelling plants were removed, lest the fruit be tainted. But the strawberry was supposed to be an exception to the rule, and was claimed to flourish in the midst of 'evil communications' without being corrupted.

The strawberry grows underneath the nettle,
And wholesome berries thrive and ripen best
Neighbour'd by fruit of baser quality;
And so the prince obscured his contemplation
Under the veil of wildness.

HENRY V (i.1)

Requirements

red twisted silk thread:
Au Ver à Soie perlée 779

red stranded thread:
DMC 321

white stranded thread:
Soie d'Alger Blanc or DMC Blanc

medium yellow stranded thread:
Madeira Silk 113 or DMC 743

dark olive stranded thread:
Soie d'Alger 2145 or DMC 469

dark green stranded thread:
Soie d'Alger 2134 or DMC 3346

red felt and paper-backed fusible web:
5 x 8 cm (3 x 2 in)

*actual size
in border*

Stems

The stems are worked in stem stitch with one strand of thread in a size 10 crewel needle.

1. Starting at the base, with dark green thread, work a row of stem stitch along the main stem line, then veer to the right where the stem divides to work the upper strawberry stem.

2. Starting at the base, with dark olive thread, work a row of stem stitch along the main stem line, on the left side of the previous row, then veer to the left where the stem divides to work the lower strawberry stem.

3. Work the upper right side stem in dark green and the left side stem in dark olive.

Leaves

The leaves are embroidered in fishbone stitch with one strand of thread. Work the lower left leaf with dark olive thread and the remaining two leaves in dark green.

1. Starting at the tip, work the leaf with close fishbone stitches, making sure the stitches start just outside the traced outline.

2. Work the leaf stalks in stem stitch.

*completed
stems & leaves*

Strawberries

1. Trace the strawberry padding outlines (one the actual size and one slightly smaller for each strawberry) onto paper-backed fusible web, then fuse to the red felt. Cut out the felt padding pieces.

2. Using one strand of red stranded thread, stab stitch the smaller shape in place inside the strawberry outline. Apply the larger shape on top (fusible web-side down) with a few small stab stitches then work a row of buttonhole stitch around the outside edge (stitches 1.5 mm apart).

3. With red twisted silk thread in a size 8 milliners needle, work a row of small (1.5 mm) back stitches around the strawberry (close to the felt), starting with five back stitches at the top of the strawberry. *These five stitches will be used for the first row of the trellis stitch covering, so make sure that they are centred.*

4. Using twisted silk thread in a size 26 or 28 tapestry needle, cover the strawberry with rows of trellis stitch, using the diagram below as a guide. Work the first row of trellis stitch into the five back stitches at the top of strawberry. At the end of each row, insert the needle through to the back (enclosing the back stitches) and bring up again slightly below, to commence the next row. The rows are worked in alternate directions to produce the desired texture. Increase or decrease stitches at the end of each row if required (I gradually increased to eight stitches across the widest part of the strawberry before decreasing to work the lower part).

5. With dark olive thread, work four chain stitches at the top of the strawberry to form the sepals.

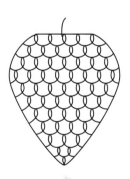

**completed
strawberry**

Strawberry Flower

1. Using one strand of white thread, work five detached chain stitches (over the marked straight lines) to act as padding for the petals.

2. Each petal is worked with about eight buttonhole stitches, radiating in a curve from the same entry point (like working a segment of a buttonhole wheel).

3. With one strand of dark green thread, work a small chain stitch between each petal.

4. Using one strand of yellow thread in a size 9 milliners needle, work the centre of the flower with French knots (one wrap).

5. Work the stem of the flower in stem stitch with dark green thread.

*completed
flower*

*actual size
in sampler*

Knapweed

The Greater Knapweed, *Centaurea scabiosa*, a
perennial member of the *Centaurea* genus, is commonly found
growing wild in hedgerows, dry grasslands and on rocky cliffs.
This plant is very valuable to bees and acts as a magnet for
many species of butterfly. The grey-green branched stems bear
single thistle-like flower heads, each having an outer ring of
long, purple-pink ragged bracts which form a crown around
the central flowers. The plant has deeply dissected leaves
which grow from the base. The pretty shapes of knapweeds
and cornflowers (both members of the *Centaurea* genus) were
popular with medieval manuscript illuminators.

The medicinal uses of cornflowers and knapweed were
well known, with at least twenty remedies being recorded.
Centaurea scabiosa has been used in traditional herbal healing,
either in the form of a soothing lotion or as an unguent for the
healing of wounds.

*Knapweed
(from Nature)*

KNAPWEED : METHOD

Requirements

purple stranded thread:
Soie d'Alger 1324 or DMC 3837

medium yellow stranded thread:
Madeira Silk 113 or DMC 743

dark green stranded thread:
Soie d'Alger 2134 or DMC 3346

medium green stranded thread:
Soie d'Alger 2133 or DMC 3347

actual size in border

Stems

The stems are worked in stem stitch with one strand of dark green thread in a size 10 crewel needle.

1. Starting at the base, work a row of stem stitch along the flower stem line to the base of the flower.

2. To work the bud stem, work a second row of stem stitch (on the left side of the first row), starting at the base, next to the first row, then left along the bud stem line.

Leaves

The leaf is embroidered in stem and split stitch with one strand of thread.

1. Using dark green thread, outline the leaf in stem stitch and work the central vein in split stitch.

2. Using medium green thread, fill the space between the central vein and the outline with rows of split stitch.

3. With dark green thread, work the lower stem leaves in stem stitch.

Knapweed Bud

The flower bud is worked with one strand of thread.

1. Using dark green thread, outline the bud with small back stitches. Work some straight stitches inside the outline to pad the bud.

2. Embroider the bud in satin stitch, enclosing the outline.

*completed
stem & leavf*

completed bud

Knapweed Flower

BASE

The flower base is worked with one strand of dark green thread.

1. Outline the base with small back stitches, leaving a small space at the top of the base. Work some straight stitches inside the outline to pad the base.

2. Embroider the base in satin stitch, enclosing the outline.

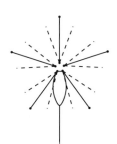

PETALS

The knapweed petals are worked in needleweaving.

1. Using two strands of purple thread in a crewel needle, stitch the 'spokes' for the needleweaving as follows, securing the thread behind the flower base as required:

- Work a straight stitch from each of the outer five dots to the points at the top of the knapweed base (five separate entry points).
- Work a slightly shorter stitch on each side of these five stitches, using the same lower entry point for each pair of stitches. There will be fifteen 'spokes' in all—one long stitch and two shorter stitches for each petal.

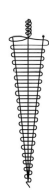

2. With one strand of purple thread in a tapestry needle, fill each group of three straight stitches with needleweaving, starting at the base and working towards the top of the petal. Weave until the ends of the shorter side stitches are reached, take the thread to the centre then wrap the end of the centre stitch (approximately four wraps) to form a point at the end of the petal. Repeat for the remaining four petals.

3. Fill the space in the centre of the knapweed with French knots using one strand of medium yellow thread in a milliners needle.

completed flower

Plum

I will dance and eat plums at your wedding.

The Merry Wives of Windsor (v.5)

Prunus domestica, the common or European Plum, is a small deciduous tree in the Rosaceae family, an ancient domesticated species that is now cultivated in temperate areas worldwide for its fruit. First recorded in cultivation by the Syrians and then the Romans, the species spread to western Europe during the Crusades. In the sixteenth century, wild plums—sloes, bullaces and blackthorn—could be found in in English hedgerows in early spring; however, it was of the domesticated plum that Gerard wrote 'my selfe have sixty sorts in my garden':

The Plum or Damson tree is of a mean bignesse, it is covered with a smooth barke: the branches are long, whereon do grow broad leaves more long than round, nicked in the edges: the floures are white; the plums do differ in colour, fashion and bignesse, they all consist of pulp and skin, and also of kernel, which is shut up in a shell or stone. Some plums are of a blackish blew, of which some be longer, others rounder, others of the colour of yellow wax, divers of a crimson red, greater for the most part than the rest.

There be also green plums, and withal very long, of a sweet and pleasant taste: more-over, the pulp or meat of some is drier, and easily separated from the stone; of other-some it is moister, and cleaveth faster. Our common Damson is known to all, and therefore not to be stood upon.

John Gerard, THE HERBALL (1597)

Bullaces and other wild plums, Bourdichon Book of Hours, *French, early 16th century*

Shakespeare made several references to plums, damsons and prunes (dried plums) in his plays:

The satirical rogue says here that old men have grey beards,
that their faces are wrinkled, their eyes purging thick amber
and plum-tree gum.

HAMLET (ii.2)

SIMPCOX: *A fall off a tree.*
WIFE: *A plum-tree, master.*
GLOUCESTER: *Mass, thou lovedst plums well that wouldst venture so.*
SIMPCOX: *Alas! Good master, my wife desired some damsons, And made me climb with danger of my life.*

HENRY VI, PART 2 (ii.1)

Three veneys for a dish of stewed prunes.

THE MERRY WIVES OF WINDSOR (i.1)

*actual size
in border*

Requirements

dark purple stranded thread:
Soie d'Alger 3326 no match in DMC

dark plum stranded thread:
Soie d'Alger 3316 no match in DMC

medium plum stranded thread:
Soie d'Alger 5116 no match in DMC

dark olive stranded thread:
Soie d'Alger 2145 or DMC 469

dark green stranded thread:
Soie d'Alger 2134 or DMC 3346

quilter's muslin:
20 cm (8 in) square

small amount of stuffing (fibre-fill) and a sate stick

Stems

The stems are worked in stem stitch with one strand of dark olive thread in a size 10 crewel needle.

1. Starting at the base, work a row of stem stitch along the main stem line, then veer to the right along the right plum stem line.

2. Starting at the base, work a second row of stem stitch on the left side of the first row, then veer to the left along the left plum stem line.

Leaves

The leaves are embroidered in fishbone stitch with one strand of thread. Work three leaves in dark olive thread and two leaves in dark green.

1. Starting at the tip, work the leaf with close fishbone stitches, making sure the stitches start just outside the traced outline.

2. Work the leaf stalks in stem stitch.

completed
stems & leaves

Plums

The plums are embroidered as slips on quilter's muslin before being cut out and applied to the main fabric.

1. Mount muslin into a 10 or 13 cm (4 or 5 in) hoop and trace both plum outlines (these are slightly larger than the design outlines to allow for the stuffing).

2. With one strand of dark purple thread, work a row of split stitch around the outline of the plum and along the curved centre line.

3. Using one strand each of dark purple, dark plum and medium plum threads, embroider the plum with long and short stitches, following the curved shape of the fruit and covering the outline. Concentrate the darker shades at the edges of the plum and the medium shades in the centre.

4. Work a row of running stitches around the plum, 2 mm from the edge, leaving two tails of thread on the front surface. Cut out the shape, leaving a small seam allowance beyond the running stitches. Take care not to cut the thread tails. Pull up the gathering stitches and finger-press the seam allowance to the wrong side.

5. Place the plum slip at the marked position and secure with tiny stab stitches, easing the edge to fit the outline and leaving a small opening at the top. It helps to make the first four stab stitches at the positions 'north, south, east and west', bringing the needle out on the traced line and inserting into the edge of the slip, then work all the way around the shape. Using a sate stick, insert a small amount of stuffing before stitching the opening closed. If necessary, work straight stitches in matching thread around the outer edge of the plum to neaten the outline. Repeat for the other plum.

completed plums

*actual size
in sampler*

76

Cornflower

The Cornflower, *Centaurea cyanus*, an annual plant with grey-green branched stems and vivid blue, pink or purple 'ragged' flowers, often grew as a weed in cornfields in the past. The pretty shapes of cornflowers and knapweeds (both members of the *Centaurea* genus) were popular with medieval manuscript illuminators, providing splashes of vivid blue, pink and purple in their decorative borders.

Cornflower Types ('Nature')

Also known as Bachelor's Button, the Cornflower was traditionally worn as a symbol of love in flirting games. It was also customary for young people to carry the flowers in their pockets, predicting their success in love, or otherwise, in proportion to the number of flowers that retained or lost their freshness. It is to this sort of foretelling that Shakespeare probably refers in *The Merry Wives of Windsor* (iii.2), where the hostess exclaims:

What say you to young Master Fenton? He capers, he dances, he has eyes of youth, he writes verses, he speaks holiday, he smells April and May; he will carry 't, he will carry 't; 'tis in his buttons; he will carry 't.

The genus *Centaurea* was named after the learned centaur Chiron of ancient Greece, who was credited with explaining the properties of plants. The medicinal uses of the genus were well known, with at least twenty remedies being recorded. Today, wild cornflower floral water, obtained by steam distillation, is used as an antiseptic to prevent eye infections and as a natural astringent. The Cornflower is edible, and is often used to add colour to salads. It is also an ingredient in some herbal teas and tea blends, and is famous in the Lady Grey blend of Twining's tea.

Requirements

medium blue stranded thread:
Soie d'Alger 4923 or DMC 798

dark blue stranded thread:
Soie d'Alger 1414 or DMC 796

old gold stranded thread:
Soie d'Alger 523 or DMC 733

dark green stranded thread:
Soie d'Alger 2134 or DMC 3346

medium green stranded thread:
Soie d'Alger 2133 or DMC 3347

<insert image A ms p 51>

actual size in border

Stems

The stems are worked in stem stitch with one strand of dark green thread in a size 10 crewel needle.

1. Work a row of stem stitch along the bud stem line.

2. Starting at the base, work a row of stem stitch along the main stem line to the base of the flower. Again starting at the base, work a second row of stem stitch next to the first.

Leaves

The leaves are embroidered in stem and split stitch with one strand of thread.

1. Using dark green thread, outline the leaf in stem stitch and work the central vein in split stitch.

2. Using medium green thread, fill the space between the central vein and the outline with rows of split stitch.

3. With dark green thread, work the lower stem leaves in stem stitch.

*completed
stems & leaves*

Cornflower Bud

The flower bud is worked with one strand of thread.

1. Using dark green thread, outline the bud with small back stitches. Work some straight stitches inside the outline to pad the bud.

*completed
bud*

2. Embroider the bud in satin stitch, enclosing the outline.

3. With one strand of medium blue thread in a size 9 milliners needle, work three French knots (one wrap) at the top of the bud.

Cornflower

BASE

The flower base is worked with one strand of dark green thread.

1. Outline the base with small back stitches, leaving a small space at the top of the base. Work some straight stitches inside the outline to pad the base.

2. Embroider the base in satin stitch, enclosing the outline.

PETALS

The cornflower petals are worked in needleweaving.

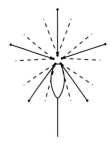

1. Using two strands of medium blue thread in a crewel needle, stitch the 'spokes' for the needleweaving as follows, securing the thread behind the flower base as required:

- Work a straight stitch from each of the outer five dots to the points at the top of the cornflower base (five separate entry points).
- Work a slightly shorter stitch on each side of these five stitches, using the same lower entry point for each pair of stitches. There will be fifteen 'spokes' in all—one long stitch and two shorter stitches for each petal.

2. With one strand of medium blue thread in a tapestry needle, fill each group of three straight stitches with needleweaving, starting at the base and working towards the top of the petal. Weave until the ends of the shorter side stitches are reached, take the thread to the centre then wrap the end of the centre stitch (approximately four wraps) to form a point at the end of the petal. Change to a milliners needle and work a French knot (one wrap) at the end of each spoke. Repeat for the remaining four petals.

3. Using one strand of dark blue thread, work a small chain stitch at the base of each petal.

4. Fill the space in the centre of the cornflower with French knots using one strand of old gold thread in a milliners needle.

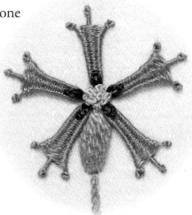

completed flower

*actual size
in sampler*

Heartsease

Yet mark'd I where the bolt of Cupid fell:
It fell upon a little western flower,
Before milk-white, now purple with love's wound,
And maidens call it Love-in-idleness.

A Midsummer Night's Dream (ii.1)

In Shakespeare's time, people believed in the power of spells, and charms, and magic potions. In *A Midsummer Night's Dream*, Oberon describes how Love-in-idleness (signifies love in vain), originally a white flower, was turned purple and given magic love potion properties, when struck by one of Cupid's arrows.

The much loved wild pansy, *Viola tricolor*, is the ancestor of all modern hybrids. Also known as Heartsease, Love-in-Idleness and Johnny-jump-ups, *Viola tricolor* grew wild in the fields and also in gardens, providing materials for lovers' potions and medical cures. Gerard describes the Heartsease with great fondness of eye:

The Hearts-ease or Pansie hath many round leaves at the first coming up; afterwards they grow somewhat longer, sleightly cut about the edges, trailing or creeping upon the ground: the stalks are weake and tender, whereupon grow floures in form & figure like the Violet, and for the most part of the same bignesse, of three sundry colours, whereof it took the syrname Trycolor, that is to say, purple, yellow, and white or blew; by reason of the beauty and braverie of which colours they are very pleasing to the eye, for smel they have little or none at all.

The Hearts-ease groweth in fields in many places, and in gardens also, and that oftentimes of it selfe: it is more gallant and beautifull than any of the wilde ones.

John Gerard, THE HERBALL (1597)

Heartsease or Viola tricolor *or Johnny Jump Up or Wild Pansy, vintage engraved illustration.* Trousset encyclopedia *(1886 – 1891).*

Viola tricolor is one of the many medicinal plants whose traditional healing properties have been confirmed by modern science, only disappearing from pharmacists' books in 1926. It was claimed, in medieval times, that 'To relieve heart trouble, collect the heads of the wild pansy (called heart-ease), boil them, and drink a wine glass full of the infusion every morning'.

*actual size
in border*

Requirements

dark lavender stranded thread:
Soie d'Alger 1343 or DMC 3746

medium lavender stranded thread:
Soie d'Alger 1342 or DMC 340

dark yellow stranded thread:
Madeira Silk 114 or DMC 742

light yellow stranded thread:
DMC 744

orange stranded thread:
DMC 741

dark purple fine silk thread:
YLI Silk Stitch 50 col. 24

dark green stranded thread:
Soie d'Alger 2134 or DMC 3346

medium green stranded thread:
Soie d'Alger 2133 or DMC 3347

ecru stranded thread:
DMC Ecru

quilter's muslin:
20 cm (8 in) square

33 gauge white covered wire (detached petals):
*ten 9 cm (3½ in) lengths; if desired, colour four lengths of
wire violet for the upper petals (Copic BV08 Blue Violet),
colour two lengths of wire yellow for the lower petals
(Copic Y15 Cadmium Yellow), and keep remaining four
lengths of wire white for the paler side petals*

Stems

The stems are worked in stem stitch with one strand of dark green thread in a size 10 crewel needle.

1. Starting at the base, work a row of stem stitch along the main stem line, then veer to the right where the stem divides to work the lower heartsease stem.

2. Starting at the base, work a row of stem stitch along the main stem line, on the left side of the previous row, then veer to the left where the stem divides to work the upper heartsease stem. Work the left side stem.

Leaves

The leaves are embroidered in buttonhole stitch with one strand of dark or medium green thread.

1. Using dark green thread, embroider both sides of the lower leaves with long buttonhole stitches, worked at an angle (the ridge of the buttonhole forms the leaf outline). When embroidering the second side of each leaf, insert the needle into the base of the buttonhole stitches of the first side to avoid a gap in the centre of the leaf. To add some contrast, work the upper side of three of the leaves in medium green thread.

2. Work the leaf stems in stem stitch with dark green thread.

completed
stems & leaves

Lower Heartsease Flower

Mount muslin into a small hoop and trace five petals for the lower heartsease and five petals for the upper heartsease. Number them from 1 to 5 as indicated. The petals are embroidered with one strand of thread in a size 10 crewel needle.

PETALS 1 & 2

1. Using one strand of dark lavender thread, and starting at the base of the petal, couch a length of wire around the petal outline, crossing the wire tails at the base (trim the 'underneath' wire to 3 mm, retaining one long wire tail with which to attach the petal). Buttonhole-stitch the wire to the muslin.

2. Using dark lavender thread, work a row of long and short buttonhole stitch inside the wire at the top edge of the petal (this row of stitching will come about halfway down the petal) then embroider the remainder of the petal in long and short stitch.

PETALS 3 & 4

1. Using one strand of medium lavender thread, couch a length of wire around the petal outline, crossing the wire tails at the base (trim the 'underneath' wire to 3 mm, retaining one long wire tail). Buttonhole-stitch the wire to the muslin.

2. Using medium lavender thread, work a row of long and short buttonhole stitch inside the wire at the top edge of the petal, then embroider the remainder of the petal in long and short stitch.

3. With one strand of dark purple silk thread in a size 12 sharps needle, work three straight stitches at the base of the petal to form rays.

PETAL 5

1. Using dark yellow thread, couch a length of wire (coloured yellow if desired) around the petal outline, leaving two wire tails, of equal length, that touch but do not cross. Buttonhole-stitch the wire to the muslin.

2. Using dark yellow thread, work a row of long and short buttonhole stitch inside the wire at the top edge of the petal, then embroider the remainder of the petal in long and short stitch.

3. With one strand of dark purple silk thread in a size 12 sharps needle, work five straight stitches (of varying lengths) at the base of the petal to form rays, leaving a small space at the inner corner of the petal.

Upper Heartsease Flower

PETALS 1 & 2

Work as for the Lower Heartsease Flower.

PETALS 3 & 4

1. Using light yellow thread, couch a length of wire around the petal outline, crossing the wire tails at the base (trim the 'underneath' wire to 3 mm, retaining one wire tail). Buttonhole-stitch the wire to the muslin.

completed lower flower

2. Using light yellow thread, work a row of long and short buttonhole stitch inside the wire at the top edge of the petal then embroider the remainder of the petal in long and short stitch.

3. With one strand of dark purple silk thread in a size 12 sharps needle, work three straight stitches at the base of the petal to form rays.

PETAL 5

Work as for the Lower Heartsease Flower.

To Complete the Heartsease

1. Carefully cut out the petals close to the buttonholed edge. For petals 1–4, trim the short wire tails close to the stitching, being careful not to cut the remaining wire tail.

2. Using a large yarn darner, insert the five Heartsease petals through one hole at the top of the stem. Apply the petals in the order as numbered (petal 5 is applied last), securing the wire tails to the muslin behind each petal with small stitches using ecru thread (it is easier to secure each petal before proceeding to the next). Separate the two wire tails for petal 5 (like an upside down V) and secure individually to stop the petal moving when finally shaped.

Do not trim the wires until the centre is worked.

3. With four strands of orange thread in a size 3 milliners needle, work the centre of each heartsease with a French knot (one loose wrap), worked into the 'hole' between the petals. Carefully shape the petals with tweezers then trim the wire tails.

*completed
upper flower*

*actual size
in sampler*

88

Redcurrant

Currants are among the most beautiful of small fruits and were very popular
in the seventeenth century. William Lawson wrote of his garden, with borders on every
side 'hanging and dropping with Feberries, Raspberries, Barberries, Currans … and
Strawberries Red White and Green'. The Redcurrant, *Ribes rubrum*, is native to parts
of western Europe. The inconspicuous yellow-green flowers mature into the bright
red translucent berries frequently used in jams and jellies. Redcurrants, glistening like
jewels, were much favoured by medieval artists to embellish illuminated manuscripts.

The English name 'currant' has been used for this fruit only since 1550. It derives from
the fruit's resemblance to the dried currants of Greece—the fruit of the small seedless
grape, *Vitis corinthiaca*. It is this currant listed by the clown in *A Winter's Tale*:

… what am I to buy for our sheep-shearing feast?
Three pound of sugar, five pound of currants, rice …
    A Winter's Tale (iv.3)

The English currants—red, black and white—are of an entirely different family,
closely allied to the Gooseberry. They do not seem to have been much grown
as garden fruit until the early part of the sixteenth century, but were known in
Shakespeare's time, for Gerard, in speaking of Gooseberries, says, 'We have also
in our London gardens another sort altogether without prickes, whose fruit is
very small, lesser by muche than the common kinde, but of a perfect red colour'.
This 'perfect red colour' explains the 'currant lip' spoken of by Theseus:

I stamp this kisse upon thy currant lippe.
    Two Noble Kinsmen (i.1)

Requirements

light red stranded thread:
Soie d'Alger 944 or DMC 321

medium red stranded thread:
Soie d'Alger 945 or DMC 498

dark red stranded thread:
Soie d'Alger 946 or DMC 815

brown stranded thread:
DMC 898

dark olive stranded thread:
Soie d'Alger 2145 or DMC 469

medium olive stranded thread:
Soie d'Alger 3733 or DMC 471

Mill Hill glass pebble beads 5025 *(ruby)*

*actual size
in border*

Stems

The stems are worked in stem stitch with one strand of dark olive thread in a size 10 crewel needle.

1. Starting at the base, work a row of stem stitch along the stem line, veering to the right at the top of the stem to work the right leaf stalk.

2. Work a row second row of stem stitch (on the left side of the first row) along the stem line, veering to the left at the top of the stem to work the left leaf stalk.

Leaves

The leaves are embroidered in buttonhole stitch with one strand of thread.

1. Using dark olive thread, embroider both sides of each leaf with long buttonhole stitches, worked at an angle (the ridge of the buttonhole forms the leaf outline). To add some contrast to the leaves, work three sides, at random, with medium olive thread. When embroidering the second side of each leaf, insert the needle into the base of the buttonhole stitches of the first side to avoid a gap in the centre of the leaf.

2. Work the remaining leaf stems in stem stitch with dark olive thread.

*completed
stems & leaves*

Redcurrants

Make two light red currants, two medium red currants and one dark red currant.

1. With one long strand of red thread (80 cm/30 in) in a size 28 tapestry needle, stitch through the hole in the pebble bead until it is smoothly covered, leaving a 10–15 cm (4–6 in) tail of thread at each side of the bead.

2. Work a tuft at the top of the bead as follows:

- Cut a 15 cm (6 in) length of brown thread (six strands). Knot the ends together to form a loop.
- Pass one of the tails of red thread (in a needle) through the brown thread loop then through the covered bead. Pull the red thread gently to pull the brown thread into the hole of the bead to form a tuft (do not cut yet). There will now be two red thread tails below the bead (these will be wrapped to form a stalk).

completed redcurrants

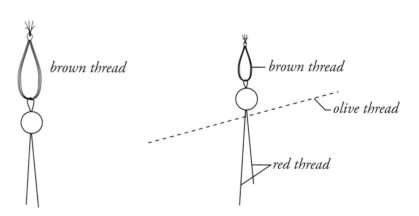

brown thread

brown thread

olive thread

red thread

3. Work a stalk below the bead as follows:

- Separate the two red thread tails and lay one strand (about 30 cm/12 in long) of medium olive thread between them (at right angles). Knot the red thread tails around the middle of the olive thread (with a square knot) to secure it at the base of the covered bead (there will now be four strands of thread at the base of the bead—two red and two olive (these will form the stalk of the currant).

- To facilitate the wrapping of the stalk, attach the loop of brown thread to a firm surface (tape to a table or pin to your knee—only your clothing!).

- To wrap the stalk, hold two red tails and one olive tail firmly in one hand then wrap these threads with the remaining strand of olive. Wrap, closely, until about 12 mm (5/8 in) in length. Secure the wrapping thread with a small knot (retain thread tails).

4. To form the tuft, trim the loop of brown thread about 2 mm away from the top of the bead. Fluff with a needle.

5. Position the redcurrants as desired, using the smallest yarn darner to insert the stalk threads through the stitched stem. Adjust the length of the stalks, allowing the redcurrants to hang loosely. Secure the stalks at the back of the stem then trim.

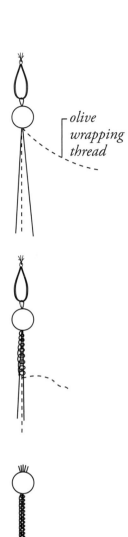

olive wrapping thread

actual size in sampler

Grapevine

What win I, if I gain the thing I seek?
A dream, a breath, a froth of fleeting joy.
Who buys a minute's mirth to wail a week?
Or sells eternity to get a toy?
For one sweet grape who will the vine destroy?
Or what fond beggar, but to touch the crown,
Would with the sceptre straight be strucken down?

The Rape of Lucrece (211–217)

The Grapevine, *Vitis vinifera*, has been cultivated for thousands of years, for both medicinal and nutritional purposes—grapes may be eaten fresh, dried to produce raisins, or processed to make wine. Gerard extolled the virtues of the Grape:

Grapes have the preheminence among the Autumne fruits, and nourish more than they all ... and they have in them little ill juice, especially when they bee thorow ripe ...

There be some Vines that bring forth grapes of a whitish or reddish yellow colour; others of a deep red, both in the outward skin, juice, and pulpe within. There be others whose grapes are of a blew colour, or something red, yet is the juice like those of the former. These grapes doe yeeld forth a white wine before they are put into the presse, and a reddish or paller wine when they are trodden with the husks, & so left to macerate or ferment, with which if they remain too long, they yeeld forth a wine of a higher colour.

He summarises his lengthy dissertation on the Vine with the following warning:

Almighty God for the comfort of mankinde ordained Wine; but decreed withall, That it should be moderately taken, for so it is wholesome and comfortable: but when measure is turned into excesse, it becommeth unwholesome, and a poyson most venomous. Besides, how little credence is to be given to drunkards it is evident; for though they be mighty men, yet it maketh them monsters, and worse than brute beats. Finally in a word to conclude; this excessive drinking of Wine dishonoreth Noblemen, beggereth the poore, and more have beene destroied by surfeiting therewith, than by the sword.

John Gerard, THE HERBALL (1597)

The Grapevine has been a great favourite with designers from time immemorial. As Herbert Cole observed in *Heraldry Decoration and Floral Forms* (1988), 'its waving lines, curling tendrils, serrated leaves and rounded fruits must have been a temptation not easily resisted to the stone or wood carver, while its opulent beauty of colour gives the tapestry weaver or embroiderer the opportunity for any degree of richness and splendid display'. Combining decoration and symbolism of many kinds, innumerable grapevines were carved in churches and painted in the margins of manuscripts, leading to the designs being called *vignettes* and the illuminators *vignetteurs*.

*actual size
in border*

Requirements

dark grape stranded thread:
Soie d'Alger 4636 or DMC 902

dark green stranded thread:
Soie d'Alger 2134 or DMC 3346

medium green stranded thread:
Soie d'Alger 2133 or DMC 3347

Mill Hill frosted glass beads 62056 *(boysenberry)*
Mill Hill frosted glass beads 60367 *(garnet)*
Mill Hill glass seed beads 00367 *(garnet)*

Stems

The stems are worked in stem stitch with one strand of thread in a size 10 crewel needle.

1. Using dark green thread, work the lower leaf stem in outline stitch and the upper leaf stem in stem stitch.

2. Starting at the base, with dark green thread, work a row of stem stitch along the main stem line, then veer to the right at the top of the stem, and change to medium green to work the right tendril. A finer line will be obtained if this tendril is worked in outline stitch. Work the lower right tendril in outline stitch with medium green thread.

3. Starting at the base, with dark green thread, work a row of stem stitch along the main stem line, on the left side of the previous row, then veer to the left at the top of the stem, and change to medium green to work the left tendril in stem stitch. Work the lower left tendril in stem stitch with medium green thread.

4. Work the grape stems in split stitch with dark green thread.

completed stem

Leaves

The leaves are embroidered in fishbone stitch with one strand of dark green thread.

1. Starting at the tip, work the centre lobe of the grape leaf with close fishbone stitches, making sure the stitches start just outside the traced outline.

2. Work the remaining two side lobes in fishbone stitch, blending into the sides of the centre lobe where they touch.

Grapes

The beads for the grapes are applied with one strand of dark grape thread in a size 10 crewel needle.

1. Make one stitch along the dotted line to establish the direction for the bunch of grapes.

2. Using the long stitch as a guide to length and direction, apply the beads, one at a time. Keep adding beads, on top of each other, until the desired shape is achieved, using a few of the shiny garnet beads for highlights.

completed leaf

completed grapes

actual size in sampler

98

Sweet Briar

Also known as Eglantine, the Sweet Briar, *Rosa rubiginosa*, is a species of rose native to Europe and western Asia. It grows as a dense shrub, two to three metres in height, with pale pink flowers borne on very thorny stems—Sweet Briar was thought by poets in Shakespeare's time to be the emblem of pleasure mixed with pain. A favourite of the Elizabethan era, where it was seen as a symbol of purity, the Eglantine was used not only in literature (there are many allusions in Elizabethan literature to the Queen as 'Eglantine') but also in dress, jewellery and paintings.

In addition to its pretty flowers, *Rosa rubiginosa* is valued in the garden for its foliage, which has a strong apple-like fragrance, and the dark red hips that remain well into the winter. A delightful description of the Sweet Briar comes from Gerard:

Sweet Briar embroidery motif (John Overton)

The sweet Brier doth oftentimes grow higher than all the kindes of Roses; the shoots of it are hard, thicke, and wooddy; the leaves are glittering, and of a beautiful greene colour, of smell most pleasant: the Roses are little, five leaved, most commonly whitish, seldom tending to purple, of little or no smell at all: the fruit is long, of colour somewhat red, like a little olive stone, & like the little heads or berries of the others ...

John Gerard, THE HERBALL (1597)

Shakespeare's fondness for wild flowers, including Eglantine, is revealed in one of the most familiar of all quotations from his plays—that of King Oberon's speech to his fairy messenger, Puck, in *A Midsummer Night's Dream* (see page 5).

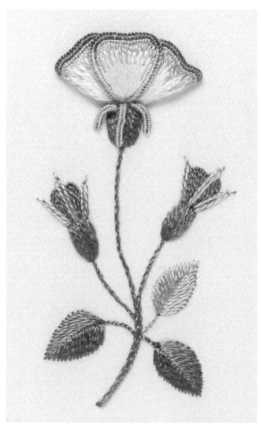

*actual size
in border*

Requirements

dark rose stranded thread:
Soie d'Alger 4634 or DMC 3726

medium rose stranded thread:
Soie d'Alger 4633 or DMC 778

pale rose stranded thread:
Soie d'Alger 4147 or DMC 225

old gold stranded thread:
Soie d'Alger 523 or DMC 733

dark olive stranded thread:
Soie d'Alger 2145 or DMC 469

medium olive stranded thread:
Soie d'Alger 3733 or DMC 471

quilter's muslin:
20 cm (8 in) square

33 gauge white covered wire (detached petals):
three 9 cm (3½ in) lengths

Stems

The stems are worked in stem stitch with one strand of dark olive thread in a size 10 crewel needle.

1. Starting at the base, work a row of stem stitch along the main stem line.

2. Starting at the base, work a second row of stem stitch on the right side of the first row then veer to the right along the right bud stem line.

3. Starting at the main stem, work a row of stem stitch along the left bud stem line.

Leaves

The leaves are embroidered in fishbone stitch with one strand of thread. Work the upper leaf in medium olive thread and the lower leaves in dark olive.

1. Starting at the tip, work the leaf with close fishbone stitches, making sure the stitches start just outside the traced outline.

2. Work the leaf stalks in stem stitch.

Sweet Briar Bud

1. Using dark rose thread, work the bud petals with long buttonhole stitches, the ridge of the stitch forming the top edge of the petals.

2. Using dark olive thread, outline the bud base with small back stitches. Work three chain stitches, inside the outline, to pad the base. Embroider the base in satin stitch, working from the stem end into the base of the petals and enclosing the outline.

*completed
stems & leaves*

completed
bud

3. The sepals are worked with detached chain stitches using one strand of medium olive thread. Work three chain stitches from the top of the base over the petals.

Sweet Briar

Background Petals

The background petals are worked with one strand of thread.

Using dark rose thread, work a row of long and short buttonhole stitch along the outer edge of both petals, working the stitches close together and keeping the stitch direction towards the base of the petals (this row of stitching will come about halfway down the petal). With medium rose thread, work a row of long and short stitch, blending into the dark rose stitches. Changing to pale rose thread, fill the petals with long and short stitch, blending into the medium rose stitches.

Base

Using dark olive thread, outline the sweet briar base with small back stitches. Work three chain stitches, inside the outline, to pad the base. Embroider the base in satin stitch, working from the stem end into the base of the petals and enclosing the outline.

Detached Petals

1. Mount the muslin into a small hoop and trace three petal outlines.

2. Using one strand of medium rose thread, couch a length of wire around the petal outline, working two couching stitches on both sides of the petal but no stitches across the top edge, as this will be worked in dark rose (the wire tails touch but do not cross). Starting with medium rose thread, buttonhole stitch the wire to the muslin along one side of the petal, stopping just before the upper corner is reached. Park the thread and change to dark rose to work the top edge of the petal. Return to the medium rose thread to buttonhole the remaining side of the petal.

3. Work a row of long and short buttonhole stitch inside the wire at the top edge of the petal with medium rose thread (this row of stitching will come about halfway down the petal). Embroider the remainder of the petal in long and short stitch in light rose thread, blending into the medium rose edge.

4. Carefully cut out the petals and select the 'best' for the centre petal. To shape the side petals, fold under the left side edge of one petal and squeeze with tweezers (this will cause the wires to cross at the base). Fold under the right side edge of the remaining side petal. Using a yarn darner, insert the right and left side petals through two holes at the top of the base. Temporarily hold the wires behind the base with masking tape. Arrange the petals, then invisibly stitch the 'fold' to the satin to keep it flat against the background. Secure the wires behind the base with tiny stitches. Do not trim the wires until the sepals have been worked.

5. Using a yarn darner, insert the centre petal at the top of the base, between the side petals. Bend the wire tails behind the embroidered background petals and secure. Shape the petals with tweezers.

side petal insertion points

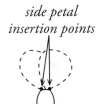

SEPALS

Using one strand of old gold thread, work three sepals at the base of the petals in needle-weaving (see Stitch Guide). Work the side sepals first then the centre sepal. Use a small crewel needle to stitch the loops and a tapestry needle to work the needle-weaving. To work a sepal:

1. Bring the needle out at the insertion point of a side petal then insert again, close by, making a loop the length of the base of the flower. Work a second loop, exactly as the first, to make the loop double (work a tiny securing stitch at the back if required). Pass a length of scrap thread through the loop to enable it to be held under tension while working the needleweaving.

2. Bring the needle out again at the base of the loop and change to a tapestry needle. Holding the loop under tension with the scrap thread, slide the needle through the centre of the loop, alternately from the right then the left, to fill the loop with needle-weaving, keeping the tension firm and even. Remove the scrap thread then insert the needle to the side of the base (below the petal), slightly shorter than the woven length—this will allow the sepal to form a curve. Secure the thread at the back. Work the other side sepal in the same way, then finally the centre sepal. Shape the petals and the sepals then trim the wires.

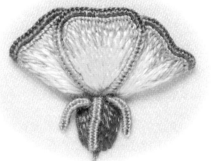

completed flower

actual size in sampler

The Border

As in the original letter, the border of flowers is outlined with pairs of fine red lines. These have been worked in back stitch with one strand of red thread in a size 10 crewel needle.

The original letter has what appears to be the letter N in each corner. I have not been able to ascertain the significance of this, but, as my surname starts with an N, I was quite happy to retain it.
You might like to experiment with a version of your own initial.

-- -- -- -- -- -- -- -- -- -- -- -- -- -- -- -- --

Requirements

variegated red stranded thread:
Threadworx Hand Overdyed Floss col.1089
or Sampler Threads from The Gentle Art col. 0360 (Cranberry)
or DMC 4210

19 mm (¾ in) Scotch Removable Magic Tape

manila folder or fine card: narrow strips
the length of the border and 2.5 mm wide

30 cm (12 in) metal ruler

The border has already been outlined with two rows of tacking (running) stitch in silk thread. Using these tacked border lines as a guide, work rows of back stitch along the border lines as follows:

1. Cut a length of Magic Tape slightly longer than the lower outer border line. Stick the tape to the satin, next to the tacked, lower outer border line, using a ruler to check that it is straight (if the tacked line is not exactly straight, this is your chance to straighten it).

Carefully unpick the line of tacking next to the tape. The edge of the tape will now be your guide for the first row of back stitch. Starting at one corner of the border, work back stitches,

approximately 2.5 mm in length, along the line of tape to the other corner (if shorter stitches are used, it is more difficult to achieve a straight line). Work the back stitches in a stabbing motion and do not pull them too tight. Secure the thread then remove the tape. Repeat for the remaining three outer border lines.

2. Work a row of back stitch along the four inner border lines in the same way.

3. Cut a strip of manila card 2.5 mm wide and slightly longer than the lower outer border line. Place this strip next to, and outside, the back stitched line. Hold the strip at each end with small pieces of masking tape. Cut a length of Magic Tape slightly longer than the lower border line. Stick the tape to the satin, next to the outside edge of this card template.

Remove the card template. The edge of the tape will now be your guide for stitching the second row of back stitches that form the outer border. Work a row of back stitches along the line of tape, making the line approximately 2.5 mm

longer at each end to allow for the corners that will be formed with the adjacent border lines (use a piece of manila card as a guide). Repeat for the remaining three outer border lines.

4. Using the same technique, work a second row of back stitch *inside* the inner border lines.

actual size in sampler

CORNER INITIALS : METHOD

Requirements

variegated red stranded thread: (as for the border lines)

19 mm (¾ in) Scotch Removable Magic Tape

The initial is worked with one strand of red thread in a size 10 crewel needle.

The wider vertical lines of the initial consist of four rows of stem stitch, worked side by side (stem stitch filling), either to the right or to the left of

the grid lines provided. The fine diagonal lines are worked in outline stitch.

I used a strip of Magic Tape above and below the grid lines to help keep the initial straight at the top and the bottom.

a   b   c   d

a   b   c   d

a   b   c   d

1. Starting at line (a), work four rows of stem stitch, to the right of this line.

2. Work a diagonal row of outline stitch from the top of the fourth row of stem stitch to the bottom of line (c).

3. Starting at line (d), work four rows of stem stitch, to the left of this line.

4. Work a diagonal row of outline stitch from the bottom of the fourth row of stem stitch to the top of line (b).

5. Starting at line (b), work four rows of stem stitch to the left of this line (over the row of outline stitch).

6. Starting at line (c), work four rows of stem stitch to the right of line (over the row of outline stitch).

7. To make the vertical lines slightly wider at the top and bottom, work a small slanted stitch on both sides, at the top and bottom of each vertical line.

8. Remove the Magic Tape from the upper and lower edges of the initial (if used). To neaten the top and bottom edges of the pairs of vertical lines, work a long stitch from (a) to (b) at the top and bottom edges. Work a second stitch over the first, then couch in the middle with a tiny couching stitch. Repeat at the top and bottom of (c) to (d).

*actual size
in sampler*

Shakespeare's Flowers

THE SAMPLERS

PART ✤ TWO

SHAKESPEARE'S FLOWERS: THE SAMPLERS

Embroidering 'A Border of Shakespeare's Flowers' was a joy
—but it was also quite a challenge. I wanted to interpret the border
of Lady Anne Clifford's letter, close to its original size, in stumpwork
and surface embroidery. At the time, I assumed that the dimensions of
the emailed image—16.6 x 24 cm (6½ x 9½ in)—were the size of the
original letter. I later discovered that the actual letter is about
10 per cent larger. While the embroidery techniques in themselves
are not difficult, working them at that small scale was!

I decided to enlarge twelve of the flowers from the Border
(the percentage of enlargement varied from flower to flower) and
combine them, in groups of four, to work as three Samplers.
As in the original letter, the Samplers are outlined with pairs of
red lines—these are worked in back stitch.

Previous page: samplers actual size. Opposite: 95% of actual size

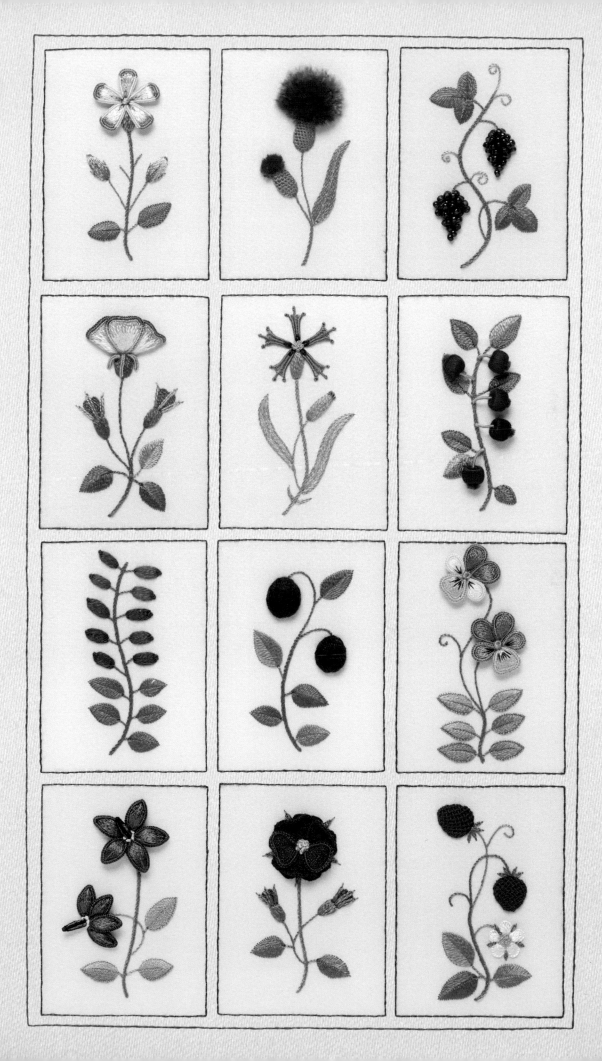

There are myriad ways that the flower panes may be arranged. The Samplers may be worked as three individual panels and framed separately, or the three panels may be mounted together in one frame.

The three original panels may be worked, side by side, as one large rectangle— six flower panes across, two flower panes deep.

Combine the twelve flower panes to form a rectangle— four flower panes across and three flower panes deep.

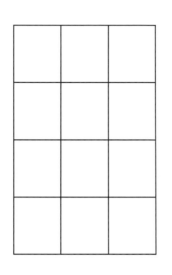

Combine the twelve flower panes to form a vertical rectangle— three flower panes across and four flower panes deep.

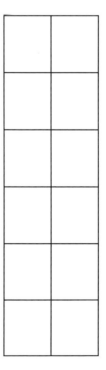

Work a vertical panel of flowers—two flower panes wide and six flower panes deep—perfect for a narrow wall space.

SAMPLER LAYOUTS (CONTINUED)

Work a narrow horizontal panel of individual flower panes—all twelve flowers or less as desired.

You may wish to include the remaining two flowers from the Border, Knapweed and Bellflower, in your Sampler (they will need to be enlarged to fit the sampler grid). You could then work a block of 15 panes—14 flower panes with, perhaps, an initial in the centre pane.

The possibilities are endless!

Hint: *Photocopy the flowers from the Samplers and cut them out as little panes. Rearrange them to get a combination that is pleasing. The flower colours may also be changed if desired.*

Individual flower panes may also be used for the covers of a needle-book.

Instead of red back stitch, the border lines could be worked in green, or could be replaced with couched gold or red thread, perhaps couched with green.

Before you begin...

The flowers in *'Shakespeare's Flowers: the Samplers'* are worked with stumpwork and surface embroidery techniques. Before you begin, it will be helpful to familiarise yourself with the following information:

❋ Read through all the instructions before commencing work on the project. As a general rule, work all surface embroidery before applying any detached elements.

❋ The diagrams in the skeleton outline of the Samplers, and the outlines for the detached elements, are actual size. The explanatory diagrams accompanying the instructions have often been enlarged for clarity.

❋ When designing the three *Shakespeare's Flowers Samplers*, I enlarged the flowers from *'A Border of Shakespeare's Flowers'* to fit the rectangular panes of the samplers. The instructions are the same as for the border.

Sampler One

This small stumpwork panel, the first in a series of three, features the Sweet Briar, *Rosa rubiginosa,* with detached petals and needle-woven sepals, a Grapevine, *Vitis Vinifera,* the grapes worked with glass beads, Heartsease, *Viola tricolor,* with detached wired petals, and Strawberries, *Fragaria vesca,* padded and covered with trellis stitch.

The panel is outlined with a border of fine red lines, worked in back stitch.

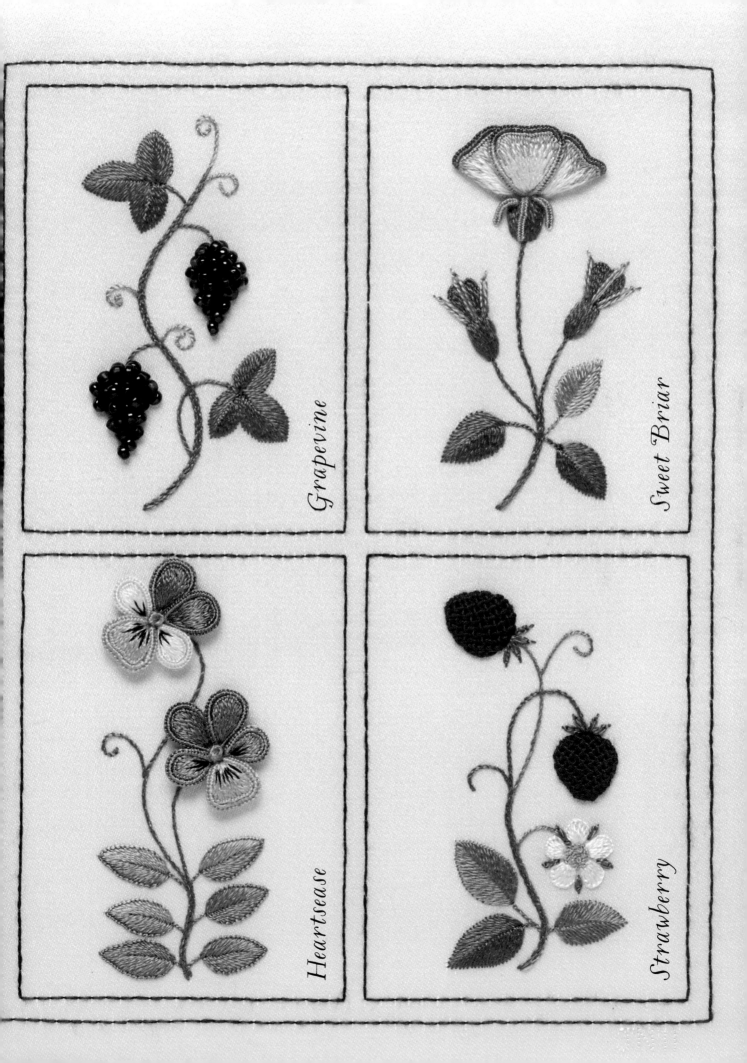

Grapevine

Sweet Briar

Heartsease

Strawberry

SAMPLER ONE DIAGRAMS

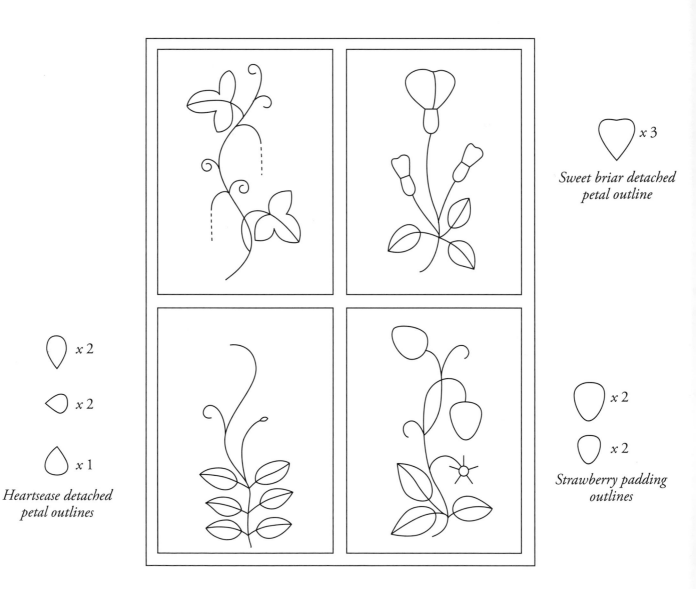

x 3

Sweet briar detached petal outline

x 2

x 2

x 1

Heartsease detached petal outlines

x 2

x 2

Strawberry padding outlines

Diagrams are actual size

OVERALL REQUIREMENTS

This is the complete list of requirements for Sampler One. For ease of use, the requirements for each individual element are repeated under its heading—for example, Sweet Briar requirements.

- -

ivory satin: *30 cm square*
quilter's muslin: *30 cm square*
quilter's muslin: *two 20 cm (8 in) squares*
red felt: *5 x 8 cm (2 x 3 in)*
paper-backed fusible web:
  5 x 8 cm (2 x 3 in)

25 cm (10 in) embroidery hoop or stretcher bars
10 or 13 cm (4 or 5 in) embroidery hoops
needles:
  crewel/embroidery sizes 5–10
  milliners/straw sizes 3–9
  sharps size 11 or 12
  tapestry sizes 26–28
  sharp yarn darners sizes 14–18
embroidery equipment (see page 244)

sharp HB lead pencil
  (or 0.5 mm clutch or mechanical pencil)
stylus, Clover Tracing Pen or empty/used
  ballpoint pen (for tracing fine lines)
15 cm ruler

tracing paper
translucent removable adhesive tape:
  13 mm (1/2 in) Scotch Removable Magic Tape
thin card or manila folder

fine silk tacking thread
  YLI Silk Stitch #100 (col.215)
ecru stranded thread: DMC Ecru

Stems & Leaves

dark olive stranded thread:
  Soie d'Alger 2145 or DMC 469
medium olive stranded thread:
  Soie d'Alger 3733 or DMC 471
dark green stranded thread:
  Soie d'Alger 2134 or DMC 3346
medium green stranded thread:
  Soie d'Alger 2133 or DMC 3347

Grape Vine

dark grape stranded thread:
  Soie d'Alger 4636 or DMC 902

Heartsease

dark lavender stranded thread:
  Soie d'Alger 1343 or DMC 3746
medium lavender stranded thread:
  Soie d'Alger 1342 or DMC 340
dark yellow stranded thread:
  Madeira Silk 114 or DMC 742
light yellow stranded thread: *DMC 744*
orange stranded thread: *DMC 741*
dark purple fine silk thread
  YLI Silk Stitch 50 col. 24

Strawberries

red twisted silk thread:
  Au ver à Soie Perlée 779
red stranded thread: *DMC 321*
white stranded thread:
  Soie d'Alger Blanc or DMC Blanc
medium yellow stranded thread:
  Madeira Silk 113 or DMC 743

Sweet Briar

dark rose stranded thread:
  Soie d'Alger 4634 or DMC 3726
medium rose stranded thread:
  Soie d'Alger 4633 or DMC 778
pale rose stranded thread:
  Soie d'Alger 4147 or DMC 225
old gold stranded thread:
  Soie d'Alger 523 or DMC 733

Border

variegated red stranded thread:
  Threadworx Hand Overdyed Floss col. 1089 or
  Sampler Threads from The Gentle Art col. 0360
  (Cranberry) or DMC 4210

Mill Hill frosted glass beads 62056 *(boysenberry)*
Mill Hill frosted glass beads 60367 *(garnet)*
Mill Hill glass seed beads 00367 *(garnet)*
33 gauge white covered wire (detached petals):
  three 9 cm (3½ in) lengths
33 gauge white covered wire (detached petals):
  ten 9 cm (3½ in) lengths
  (colour two wires yellow for the lower petals if
  desired, Copic Y15 Cadmium Yellow)

1. Mount the satin background fabric and the muslin backing into the 25 cm (10 in) embroidery hoop or frame. Pull both layers as tight as a drum, taking care not to distort the grain of the fabric. The fabrics will not be removed from the frame until the embroidery is complete.

2. Using a fine lead pencil, trace the skeleton outlines of the design and border onto tracing paper. This will be the 'right side' of the tracing paper. Flip the tracing paper over and draw over the *design outlines only* on the back (not the border lines). If necessary, trim excess tracing paper so that the traced design fits inside the back of the hoop of fabric.

3. Position the 'right side' of the tracing paper against the muslin backing fabric (inside the back of the hoop), checking that the border lines are aligned with the straight grain of the satin at the front. Temporarily secure the tracing paper with strips of masking tape. Using a stylus, draw over the border lines to transfer the outlines to the muslin backing.

4. Using fine thread, tack the outside border line to facilitate the tracing of the design to the front. Make the stitches large as they will be removed after the tracing is complete.

5. With the tracing paper 'right side up', position the tracing over the satin, lining up the traced border lines with the tacked border lines. Temporarily secure the edges of the tracing paper to the satin with strips of masking tape. Using a stylus, draw over the design lines to transfer the skeleton outline of the design to the satin (it helps to have a board underneath the frame of fabric to provide a firm surface). Remove the large border tacking stitches.

6. With fine silk thread in a size 12 sharps needle and using the traced border lines on the back, work a row of smaller tacking/running stitches along all the border lines. Make the stitches about 1 cm long on the front (short on the back) and work a back stitch into each corner. These stitches (which will eventually be removed) will be used as a guide when working the red back stitch lines for the border.

SAMPLER ONE: METHOD

Embroider each flower following the individual instructions.

Grapevine
(see instructions on page 94)

Heartsease
(see instructions on page 82)

Strawberry
(see instructions on page 62)

Sweet Briar
(see instructions on page 99)

Border Lines

The border lines are worked when the flowers have been completed.

SAMPLER BORDER LINES: METHOD

As in the original letter, the sampler is outlined with pairs of fine red lines, worked in back stitch.

Requirements

variegated red stranded thread:
Threadworx Hand Overdyed Floss col.1089 or Sampler Threads from The Gentle Art col. 0360 (Cranberry) or DMC 4210

translucent removable tape:
13 mm (½ in) Scotch Removable Magic Tape

manila folder or fine card:
narrow strips the length of the border and 2.5 mm wide

narrow 15 cm (6 in) metal ruler

The border lines are worked in back stitch with one strand of red thread in a size 10 crewel needle.

The border has already been outlined with rows of tacking (running) stitch in silk thread. Using these tacked lines as a guide, work rows of back stitch along all the border lines as follows:

1. Cut a length of Magic Tape slightly longer than the lower outer border line. Stick the tape to the satin next to the tacked lower border line, using a ruler to check that it is straight (if the tacking line is not exactly straight, this is your chance to straighten it). Carefully unpick the line of tacking next to the tape. The edge of the tape will now be your guide for the first row of back stitch. Starting at one corner of the border, work back stitches, approximately 2.5 mm in length, along the line of tape to the other corner (if shorter stitches are used, it is more difficult to achieve a straight line). Work the back stitches in a stabbing motion and do not pull them too tight. Secure the thread then remove the tape. Repeat for the remaining three outer border lines

2. Cut a strip of manila card 2.5 mm wide and slightly longer than the border line. Place this strip in the space between the back stitched lower border line and the remaining lower inner lines of tacking. Hold the strip at each end with small pieces of masking tape. Cut a length of Magic Tape slightly longer than the lower outside border line. Stick the tape to the satin next to the upper edge of this card template (it should line up with the remaining inner lines of tacking).

Remove the card template and unpick the remaining short lines of tacking. The edge of the tape will now be your guide for the second row of back stitches (two shorter lines with a gap in the middle). Starting at a corner, work a row of back stitch along the first short line, stopping at the gap. Secure the thread at the back. Rejoin the thread to work the second short line (do not carry the red thread across the back—it may show).

Sampler Two

This small stumpwork panel, the second in a series of three,

is embroidered on ivory satin with silk threads. Sampler Two features the

Apothecary Rose, *Rosa gallica,* its raised petals worked in detached buttonhole

stitch, a Cornflower, *Centaurea cyanus,* with petals worked in needleweaving,

Borage, *Borago officinalis,* with embroidered detached anther and petals,

and Redcurrants, *Ribes rubrum,* the currants worked with wrapped beads.

The panel is outlined with a border of fine red lines, worked in back stitch.

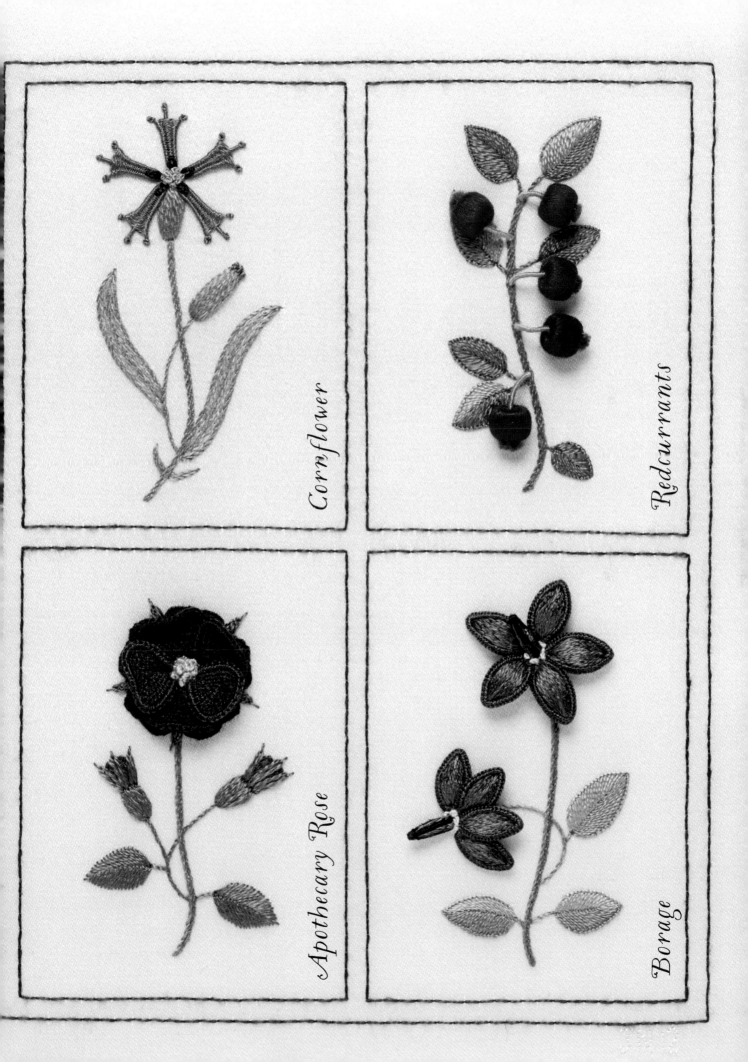

Cornflower

Redcurrants

Apothecary Rose

Borage

Rose detached
petal outline

Borage detached
petal outlines

Borage anther outline

Diagrams are actual size

OVERALL REQUIREMENTS

This is the complete list of requirements for Sampler Two. For ease of use, the requirements for each individual element are repeated under its heading—for example, Rose requirements.

ivory satin:
  30 cm (12 in) square
quilter's muslin:
  30 cm (12 in) square
quilter's muslin:
  two 20 cm (8 in) squares
red felt:
  5 x 8 cm (2 x 3 in)
paper-backed fusible web:
  5 x 8 cm (2 x 3 in)

25 cm (10 in) embroidery hoop or stretcher bars
10 or 13 cm (4 or 5 in) embroidery hoops
needles:
  crewel/embroidery sizes 5–10
  milliners/straw sizes 3–9
  sharps size 11 or 12
  tapestry sizes 26–28
  sharp yarn darners sizes 14–18
embroidery equipment (see page 244)

sharp HB lead pencil (or a 0.5mm clutch or mechanical pencil)
stylus, Clover Tracing Pen or empty/used
  ballpoint pen (for tracing fine lines)
15 cm (6 in) ruler
tracing paper
thin card or manila folder
translucent removable adhesive tape:
  13 mm (½ in) Scotch Removable Magic Tape
clear self-adhesive plastic (used for covering books):
  5 cm (2 in) squares

fine silk tacking thread:
  YLI Silk Stitch #100 (col. 215)
machine sewing thread:
  any colour that contrasts with the wine colour
ecru stranded thread: *DMC Ecru*

Overall Requirements (continued)

Stems & Leaves

dark olive stranded thread:
  Soie d'Alger 2145 or DMC 469
medium olive stranded thread:
  Soie d'Alger 3733 or DMC 471
dark green stranded thread:
  Soie d'Alger 2134 or DMC 3346
medium green stranded thread:
  Soie d'Alger 2133 or DMC 3347

Apothecary Rose

dark wine stranded thread:
  Soie d'Alger 3046 or DMC 902
medium wine stranded thread:
  Soie d'Alger 3045 or DMC 3802
medium yellow stranded thread:
  Madeira Silk 113 or DMC 743

Borage

dark blue-violet stranded thread:
  Soie d'Alger 4915 or DMC 791
medium blue-violet stranded thread:
  Soie d'Alger 4914 or DMC 158
white stranded thread:
  Soie d'Alger Blanc or DMC Blanc
black stranded thread:
  Cifonda Art Silk Black or DMC 310
dark grey stranded thread:
  Cifonda Art Silk 215 or DMC 317

Cornflower

medium blue stranded thread:
  Soie d'Alger 4923 or DMC 798
dark blue stranded thread:
  Soie d'Alger 1414 or DMC 796
old gold stranded thread:
  Soie d'Alger 523 or DMC 733

Redcurrants

light red stranded thread:
  Soie d'Alger 944 or DMC 321
medium red stranded thread:
  Soie d'Alger 945 or DMC 498
dark red stranded thread:
  Soie d'Alger 946 or DMC 815
brown stranded thread: *DMC 898*

Border

variegated red stranded thread:
  Threadworx Hand Overdyed Floss col.1089
  or Sampler Threads from The Gentle Art
  col. 0360 (Cranberry) or DMC 4210

Mill Hill glass pebble beads 5025 *(ruby)*
33 gauge white covered wire (detached petals):
  five 9 cm (3½ in) lengths
  (colour wine if desired, Copic R59 Cardinal)
33 gauge white covered wire (detached petals):
  twelve 9 cm (3½ in) lengths
  (colour blue if desired, Copic BV08 Blue Violet)

PREPARATION

1. Mount the satin background fabric and the muslin backing into the 25 cm (10 in) embroidery hoop or frame. Pull both layers as tight as a drum, taking care not to distort the grain of the fabric. The fabrics will not be removed from the frame until the embroidery is complete.

2. Using a fine lead pencil, trace the skeleton outlines of the design and border onto tracing paper. This will be the 'right side' of the tracing paper. Flip the tracing paper over and draw over the *design outlines only* on the back (not the border lines). If necessary, trim excess tracing paper so that the traced design fits inside the back of the hoop of fabric.

3. Position the 'right side' of the tracing paper against the muslin backing fabric (inside the back of the hoop), checking that the border lines are aligned with the straight grain of the satin at the front. Temporarily secure the tracing paper with strips of masking tape. Using a stylus, draw over the border lines to transfer the outlines to the muslin backing.

4. Using fine thread, tack the outside border line to facilitate the tracing of the design to the front. Make the stitches large as they will be removed after the tracing is complete.

5. With the tracing paper 'right side up', position the tracing over the satin, lining up the traced border lines with the tacked border lines. Temporarily secure the edges of the tracing paper to the satin with strips of masking tape. Using a stylus, draw over the design lines to transfer the skeleton outline of the design to the satin (it helps to have a board underneath the frame of fabric to provide a firm surface). Remove the large border tacking stitches.

6. With fine silk thread in a size 12 sharps needle and using the traced border lines on the back, work a row of smaller tacking/running stitches along all the border lines. Make the stitches about 1 cm long on the front (short on the back) and work a back stitch into each corner. These stitches (which will eventually be removed) will be used as a guide when working the red back stitch lines for the border.

SAMPLER TWO: METHOD

Embroider each flower following the individual instructions.

Apothecary Rose
(see instructions on page 30)

Borage
(see instructions on page 37)

Strawberries
(see instructions on page 62)

Cornflower
(see instructions on page 77)

Border Lines
(see instructions on page 123)

The border lines are worked when the flowers have been completed.

The Rose looks fair, but fairer we it deem

For that sweet odour that doth in it live.

The canker-blooms have full as deep a dye

As the perfumed tincture of the Roses,

Hang on such thorns, and play as wantonly

When summer's breath their masked buds discloses;

But, for their virtue only is their show,

They live unwoo'd and unrespected fade;

Die to themselves. Sweet Roses do not so;

Of their sweet deaths are sweetest odours made.

Sonnet 54

Sampler Three

This small stumpwork sampler is the third in this series. Embroidered on ivory satin with silk threads, this design features the Gillyflower, *Dianthus caryophyllus*, its padded base covered with detached buttonhole stitch and petals worked in Turkey knots, a Periwinkle, *Vinca minor*, with detached wired petals, Plums, *Prunus domestica*, embroidered and appliquéd, and Barberries, *Berberis vulgaris*, worked in padded satin stitch.
The panel is outlined with a border of fine red lines, worked in back stitch.

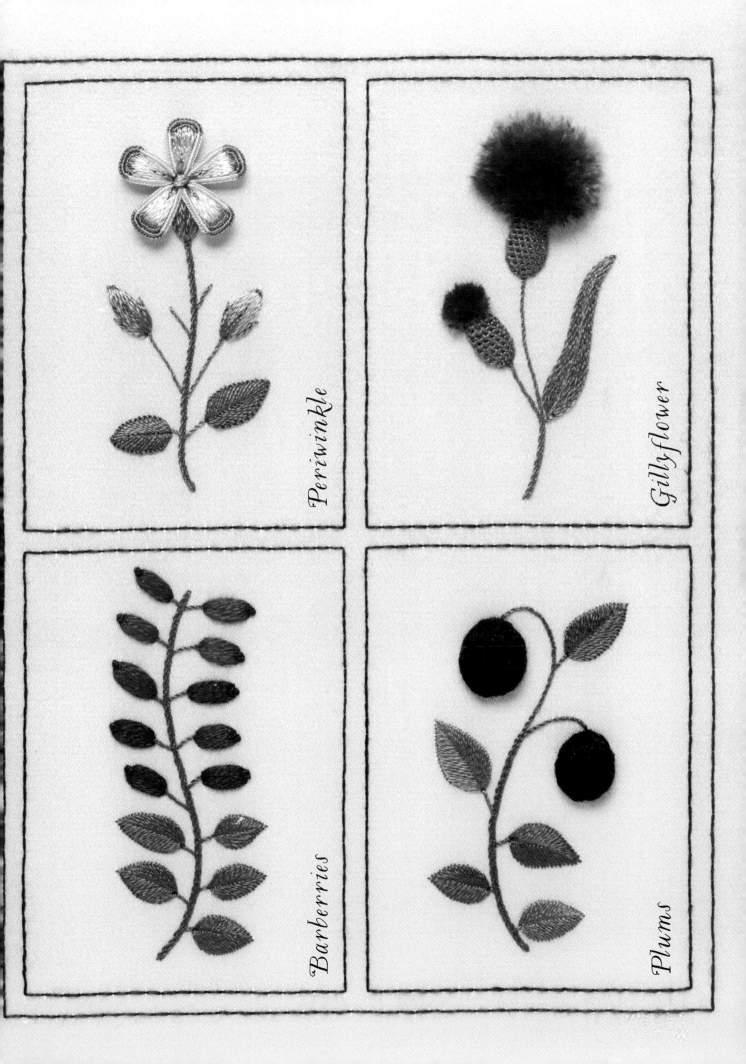

Periwinkle

Gillyflower

Barberries

Plums

Periwinkle detached petal outline

Gillyflower base padding outlines

Gillyflower bud padding outlines

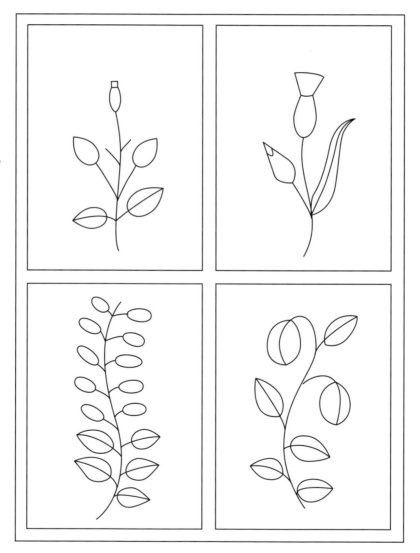

Plum outlines

Diagrams are actual size

OVERALL REQUIREMENTS

This is the complete list of requirements for Sampler Three. For ease of use, the requirements for each individual element are repeated under its heading—for example, Gillyflower requirements.

ivory satin:
   30 cm (12 in) square
quilter's muslin:
   30 cm (12 in) square
quilter's muslin:
   two 20 cm (8 in) squares
grey felt:
   5 x 8 cm (2 x 3 in)
paper-backed fusible web:
   5 x 8 cm (2 x 3 in)

---

25 cm (10 in) embroidery hoop or stretcher bars
10 or 13 cm (4 or 5 in) embroidery hoops
needles:
   crewel/embroidery sizes 5–10
   milliners/straw sizes 3–9
   sharps size 11 or 12
   tapestry sizes 26–28
   sharp yarn darners sizes 14–18
embroidery equipment (see page 244)

stylus, Clover Tracing Pen
   or empty/used ballpoint pen (for tracing fine lines)
15 cm (6 in) ruler

---

tracing paper
translucent removable adhesive tape:
   13 mm (1/2 in) Scotch Removable Magic Tape
thin card or manila folder
small amount of stuffing (fibre-fill) and a sate stick

---

fine silk tacking thread:
   YLI Silk Stitch #100 (col. 215)
ecru stranded thread: *DMC Ecru*

Stems & Leaves

dark olive stranded thread:
  Soie d'Alger 2145 or DMC 469
medium olive stranded thread:
  Soie d'Alger 3733 or DMC 471
dark green stranded thread:
  Soie d'Alger 2134 or DMC 3346
medium green stranded thread:
  Soie d'Alger 2133 or DMC 3347

Gillyflower

dark coral stranded thread:
  Soie d'Alger 2916 or DMC 347
medium coral stranded thread:
  Soie d'Alger 2915 or DMC 3328

Periwinkle

light sky-blue stranded thread:
  Cifonda Art Silk 984 or DMC 162
medium sky-blue stranded thread:
  Cifonda Art Silk 987 or DMC 826
medium yellow stranded thread:
  Madeira Silk 113 or DMC 743

Plums

dark purple stranded thread:
  Soie d'Alger 3326 no match in DMC
dark plum stranded thread:
  Soie d'Alger 3316 no match in DMC
medium plum stranded thread:
  Soie d'Alger 5116 no match in DMC

Barberries

medium orange stranded thread:
  Soie d'Alger 645 or DMC 946
dark orange stranded thread:
  Soie d'Alger 636 or DMC 900
russet stranded thread:
  Soie d'Alger 2636 or DMC 919
rust stranded thread:
  Soie d'Alger 2626 or DMC 400

Border

variegated red stranded thread:
  Threadworx Hand Overdyed Floss col. 1089
  or Sampler Threads from The Gentle Art
  col. 0360 (Cranberry) or DMC 4210

33 gauge white covered wire (detached petals):
five 9 cm (3½ in) lengths

1. Mount the satin background fabric and the muslin backing into the 25 cm (10 in) embroidery hoop or frame. Pull both layers as tight as a drum, taking care not to distort the grain of the fabric. The fabrics will not be removed from the frame until the embroidery is complete.

2. Using a fine lead pencil, trace the skeleton outlines of the design and border onto tracing paper. This will be the 'right side' of the tracing paper. Flip the tracing paper over and draw over the *design outlines only* on the back (not the border lines). If necessary, trim excess tracing paper so that the traced design fits inside the back of the hoop of fabric.

3. Position the 'right side' of the tracing paper against the muslin backing fabric (inside the back of the hoop), checking that the border lines are aligned with the straight grain of the satin at the front. Temporarily secure the tracing paper with strips of masking tape. Using a stylus, draw over the border lines to transfer the outlines to the muslin backing.

4. Using fine thread, tack the outside border line to facilitate the tracing of the design to the front. Make the stitches large as they will be removed after the tracing is complete.

5. With the tracing paper 'right side up', position the tracing over the satin, lining up the traced border lines with the tacked border lines. Temporarily secure the edges of the tracing paper to the satin with strips of masking tape. Using a stylus, draw over the design lines to transfer the skeleton outline of the design to the satin (it helps to have a board underneath the frame of fabric to provide a firm surface). Remove the large border tacking stitches.

6. With fine silk thread in a size 12 sharps needle and using the traced border lines on the back, work a row of smaller tacking/running stitches along all the border lines. Make the stitches about 1 cm long on the front (short on the back) and work a back stitch into each corner. These stitches (which will eventually be removed) will be used as a guide when working the red back stitch lines for the border.

Sampler Three: method

- -

Embroider each flower following the individual instructions.

Gillyflower

(see instructions on page 56)

Periwinkle

(see instructions on page 43)

Plum

(see instructions on page 72)

Barberry

(see instructions on page 52)

Border Lines

(see instructions on page 123)

The border lines are worked when the flowers have been completed.

ELIZABETHAN
Flower
Panel

PART THREE

Elizabethan Flower Panel

This piece was inspired by an early seventeenth-century
English embroidered panel, worked in coloured silks and metal threads,
held in the collection of the Embroiderers' Guild in the UK.

Worked on a background of ivory satin, in stumpwork and surface
embroidery, this design features flowers popular in Elizabethan times:
the Bluebell, with raised upper petals, a Crab Apple, with detached
petals and applied buds, the Honeysuckle, with slender, padded and
raised petals, Pea Pods, with detached shells and beaded peas,
a Primrose and bud, both with raised petals, and a traditional red Rose,
all enclosed by coiling stems, whipped with gold thread.

Nestled among the foliage can be found a bee, with raised wings and
velvety body, a plump caterpillar and a tiny ladybird with detached
wings. Gold spangles complete this design.

Opposite: not actual size (enlarged by 185%)

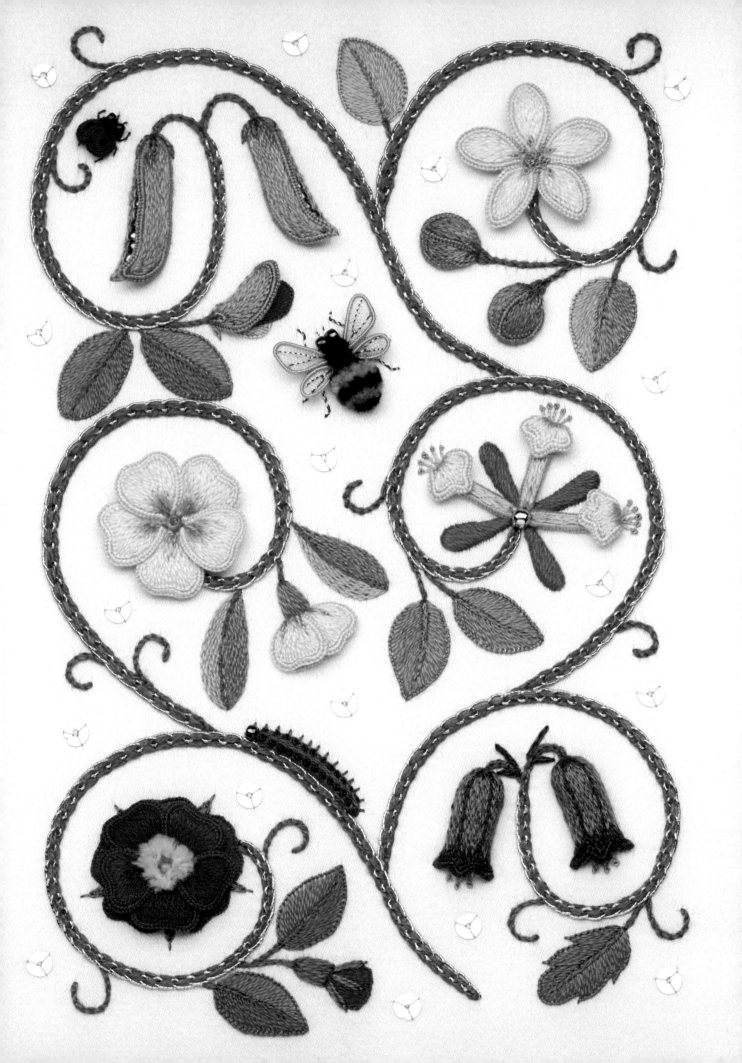

EXAMPLES OF
17TH CENTURY EMBROIDERY

Embroidered panel, possibly from a coif, English, early 17th century.
Linen embroidered with a scrolling pattern in silver-gilt thread, the flowers, animals and
birds in varied techniques including plaited braid, chain and detached needlelace stitches
in silk with metal strip and spangles. The embroidery is highly textural: the top layer of
the pea pod peels back to reveal golden peas, and some of the flowers are worked over
padding while others, and the bee's wings, are detached. EG.1982.79

Early 17th Century Coif

Linen ground fabric embroidered with silk, silver gilt threads, silver strips and spangles. Stems are worked in plaited chain. Flowers are embroidered in detached lacework. EG.16

Given to the Embroiderers Guild Collection by Mary Cayley.

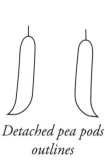

Detached pea pods
outlines

Detached crab apple
flower petal outline

Detached peaflower
petal outline

Detached crabapple
bud outline

Fore wing

Hind wing

Detached bee
wing outlines

Detached primrose
flower petal outline

Crabapple bud
padding outlines

Detached ladybird
wing outline

Detached primrose
bud petal outline

wire
insertion
points

Honeysuckle detached
petal outline

Detached rose
petal outline

Detached upper
bluebell outline

Diagrams are actual size

Skeleton outline

Diagram is actual size

OVERALL REQUIREMENTS

This is the complete list of requirements for this piece. For ease of use, the requirements for each individual element are repeated under its heading—for example, Bluebell requirements.

ivory silk satin:
 35 cm (14 in) square
quilter's muslin:
 35 cm (14 in) square
tracing paper
quilter's muslin:
 six 20 cm (8 in) squares
red cotton fabric (homespun):
 15 cm (6 in) square
honey mottled organza:
 15 cm (6 in) square
pearl metal organdie:
 15 cm (6 in) square
white felt:
 5 x 8 cm (2 x 3 in)
paper-backed fusible web:
 5 x 8 cm (2 x 3 in)

28 cm (11 in) embroidery hoop or
stretcher bars
10, 13 and 15 cm (4, 5 and 6 in)
embroidery hoops
needles:
 crewel/embroidery sizes 5–10
 milliners/straw sizes 3–9
 sharps size 11 or 12
 tapestry sizes 26–28
 sharp yarn darners sizes 14–18
embroidery equipment (see page 244)

fine silk thread:
 YLI Silk Stitch #100 (col. 215)
nylon clear thread:
 Madeira Monofil 60 col. 1001
ecru stranded thread: *DMC Ecru*

Stems & Leaves

gold couching thread 371

dark leaf-green stranded thread:
  Soie d'Alger 2126 or DMC 937

medium leaf-green stranded thread:
  Soie d'Alger 2125 or DMC 469

light leaf-green stranded thread:
  Soie d'Alger 2124 or DMC 470

dark pea-green stranded thread:
  Soie d'Alger 1834 or DMC 367

medium pea-green stranded thread:
  Soie d'Alger 1833 or DMC 368

Bluebell

dark blue stranded thread:
  Soie d'Alger 4916 or DMC 791

medium blue stranded thread:
  Soie d'Alger 4914 or DMC 158

dark yellow stranded thread:
  Soie d'Alger 545 or DMC 742

Crab Apple

medium pink stranded thread:
  Soie d'Alger 1012 or DMC 761

light pink stranded thread:
  Soie d'Alger 1011 or DMC 3713

very pale pink stranded thread:
  Soie d'Alger 3041 or DMC 819

dark coral stranded thread:
  Soie d'Alger 2915 or DMC 3712

medium coral stranded thread:
  Soie d'Alger 2914 or DMC 760

dark yellow stranded thread:
  Soie d'Alger 545 or DMC 742

lime-green stranded thread:
  Soie d'Alger 2143 or DMC 166

Honeysuckle

dark orange stranded thread:
  Soie d'Alger 913 or DMC 350

light orange stranded thread:
  Soie d'Alger 643 or DMC 3825

pale yellow stranded thread:
  Soie d'Alger 621 or DMC 3855

dark yellow stranded thread:
  Soie d'Alger 545 or DMC 742

lime-green stranded thread:
  Soie d'Alger 2143 or DMC 166

Pea Pods

dark pea-green stranded thread:
 Soie d'Alger 1834 or DMC 367
medium pea-green stranded thread:
 Soie d'Alger 1833 or DMC 368
magenta stranded thread:
 Soie d'Alger 1043 or DMC 3886 (closest match)
medium mauve stranded thread:
 Soie d'Alger 3312 or DMC 554
light mauve stranded thread:
 Soie d'Alger 3311 or DMC 153

Primrose

dark yellow stranded thread:
 Soie d'Alger 545 or DMC 742
medium yellow stranded thread:
 Soie d'Alger 542 or DMC 744

Lancaster Rose

dark red stranded thread:
 Soie d'Alger 1016 or DMC 304
medium red stranded thread:
 Soie d'Alger 1015 or DMC 321
medium yellow stranded thread:
 Soie d'Alger 542 or DMC 744

Bee

old gold stranded thread: *DMC 783*
black stranded thread: *DMC 310*
gold/black metallic thread: *Kreinik Cord 205c*
gold rayon machine thread: *Madeira Rayon 1055*

Caterpillar

russet stranded thread: *DMC 920*
dark blue stranded thread: *DMC 791*

Ladybird

black stranded thread: *DMC 310*
red stranded thread: *DMC 349*
black metallic thread: Kreinik Cord 005c

Mill Hill petite beads 42014 *(black)*
Mill Hill glass beads 374 *(oilslick)*
Mill Hill frosted glass beads 62049 *(green)*
Mill Hill antique glass beads 3037 *(abalone)*
2.5 mm gold bead
4 mm gold spangles

33 gauge white covered wire (detached petals):
 fifteen 9 cm (3½ in) lengths
33 gauge white covered wire (detached bluebells):
 *two 9 cm (3½ in) lengths (colour wires blue if
 desired, Copic BV08 Blue Violet)*
33 gauge white covered wire (detached
honeysuckle petals):
 three 12 cm (5 in) lengths
33 gauge white covered wire (detached pods):
 *two 12 cm (4½ in) lengths (colour wires Pea
 Green
 if desired, Copic YG63 Pea Green)*
33 gauge white covered wire (ladybird):
 *10 cm (4 in) length (colour red if desired,
 Copic R17 Lipstick Orange)*
28 gauge silver uncovered wire (bee wings):
 three 10 cm (4 in) lengths

1. Mount the satin background fabric and the muslin backing into the 28 cm (11 in) embroidery hoop or frame. The fabrics need to be kept very taut.

2. Cut a rectangle of thin card or paper, 10 x 15 cm (4 x 6 in). Place the rectangle template onto the satin (checking that it is aligned with the straight grain of the fabric) and hold with small pieces of Magic Tape. Using fine silk or rayon machine thread in a sharps needle, work a row of long running stitches around the rectangle (this will be used as a reference grid when transferring the skeleton design outline). Remove the card. The running stitches will be removed when the embroidery is complete.

3. Using a fine lead pencil, trace the skeleton outline of the design (including the rectangle outline) onto tracing paper. This will be the 'right side' of the tracing paper. Flip the tracing paper over and draw over the *design outlines only* on the back (not the rectangle lines).

4. With the tracing paper 'right side up', position the tracing over the satin, lining up the traced rectangle with the tacked rectangle lines. Temporarily secure the edges of the tracing paper to the satin with strips of masking tape. Using a stylus, draw over the design lines to transfer the skeleton outline of the design to the satin (it helps to have a board underneath the frame of fabric to provide a firm surface).

Note: Take care to use the minimum amount of lead when tracing. If your outlines are too dark, gently press the traced outlines with pieces of masking tape or Magic Tape to remove any excess graphite.

Order of Work

1. Coiling Stems & Tendrils

2. Pea Pods & Pea Flower

3. Ladybird

4. Crab Apple

5. Bee

6. Caterpillar

7. Primrose

8. Honeysuckle

9. Lancaster Rose

10. Bluebells

11. Spangles

Requirements

dark leaf-green stranded thread:
Soie d'Alger 2126 or DMC 937

gold couching thread 371

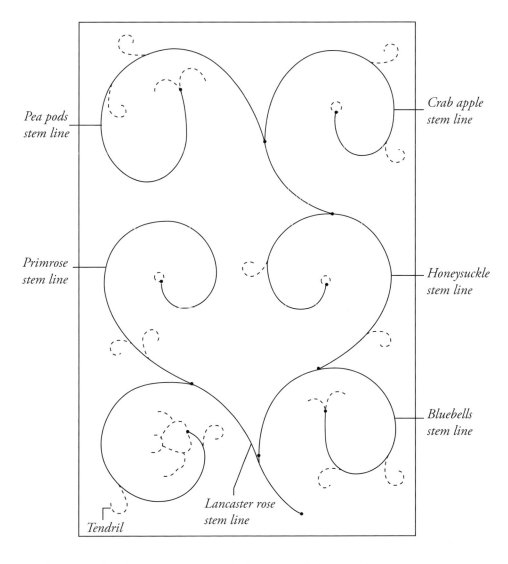

Pea pods
stem line

Crab apple
stem line

Primrose
stem line

Honeysuckle
stem line

Bluebells
stem line

Tendril

Lancaster rose
stem line

Reference only, diagram not actual size. See skeleton outline on page 145.

Coiling Stems

The coiling main stems, which enclose the flowers, are worked in interlaced chain stitch, lacing only one side of the chain stitch with gold thread. The curled tendrils, and the short stems to the flowers and leaves, are stitched at a later stage.

1. Using three strands of dark leaf-green thread in a size 5 crewel needle, work a row of broad chain stitch (see page 251) along the Lancaster Rose coiled stem line. Starting at the base, work the stitches 2.5–3 mm long, with a gap of 1 mm between the entry and exit points of the needle (use the eye of the needle to slide the thread through the loop of the previous chain stitch). Finish the stitching at the edge of the background petals of the rose.

2. With a length of gold couching thread in a size 24 tapestry needle, lace the curved outer edge of the row of broad chain stitch, following the instructions for interlaced chain stitch (see page 252).

completed stem

3. Work a row of broad chain stitch along the bluebells main stem line, starting next to the rose stem line and finishing where the stem divides to go to the bluebells (the short stems to the bluebells will be worked later). Lace the curved outer edge of the row of broad chain stitch.

4. Work a row of broad chain stitch along the primrose stem line, starting next to the rose stem line and finishing at the edge of the primrose centre circle. Lace the curved outer edge of the row of broad chain stitch.

5. Work a row of broad chain stitch along the honeysuckle stem line, starting next to the bluebell stem line and finishing at the edge of the honeysuckle centre circle. Lace the curved outer edge of the row of broad chain stitch.

6. Work a row of broad chain stitch along the pea pods main stem line, starting next to the honeysuckle stem line and finishing where the stem divides to go to the pea pods (the short stems to the pea pods will be worked later). Lace the curved outer edge of the row of broad chain stitch.

7. Work a row of broad chain stitch along the crab apple stem line, starting next to the pea pods stem line and finishing at the edge of the crab apple centre circle. Lace the curved outer edge of the row of broad chain stitch.

Tendrils

Work the curled tendrils in stem stitch, using two strands of dark leaf-green thread in a size 8 crewel needle.

completed tendril

Flower and Leaf Stems

The remaining flower and leaf stems will be stitched when working each flower.

Pea Pods

I remember the wooing of a peasecod
instead of her.

As You Like It (ii.4)

The garden Pea, *Pisum sativum*, is the cultivated form of a plant originating in the south of Europe. The Pea was known as Pease (plural Peason) in sixteenth-century England, where it became popular as a garden vegetable. In Queen Elizabeth's time peas were brought from Holland, and were renowned as 'fit dainties for ladies, they came so far and cost so dear' (Thomas Fuller).

There is a curious amount of folklore connected with Peas and Peasecods, much of it to do with love divination (the Peasecod is the ripe shell of the Pea before it is shelled). A practice called 'peasecod wooing' was widespread. A girl, when shelling green peas, would keep a close look out for a pod containing nine peas. If she chanced to find one, she would hang it over the kitchen doorway in the belief that the first man who entered was destined to be her future husband. Another popular method of 'divination by peasecod' involved a young man selecting a peasecod still growing on the stem, snatching it away quickly, and, if the peas remained intact in the shell (a good omen), in then presenting it to the lady of his choice. Shakespeare alludes to this piece of popular folklore in *As You Like It*.

Pea Pod embroidery motifs
(Richard Shorleyker)

In *Twelfth Night*, Cesario is compared to an undeveloped peapod (a squash), when Malvolio implies that he isn't quite *ripe* enough to be a man:

Not yet old enough to be a man, nor young enough for a boy; as a squash is before 'tis a peasecod, or a codling when 'tis almost an apple.

    TWELFTH NIGHT (i.5)

not actual size

Requirements

dark pea-green stranded thread:
Soie d'Alger 1834 or DMC 367

medium pea-green stranded thread:
Soie d'Alger 1833 or DMC 368

magenta stranded thread:
Soie d'Alger 1043 or DMC 3886 (closest match)

medium mauve stranded thread:
Soie d'Alger 3312 or DMC 554

light mauve stranded thread:
Soie d'Alger 3311 or DMC 153

dark leaf-green stranded thread:
Soie d'Alger 2126 or DMC 937

medium leaf-green stranded thread:
Soie d'Alger 2125 or DMC 469

nylon clear thread:
Madeira Monofil 60 col. 1001

quilter's muslin:
20 cm (8 in) square in a 10 cm (4 in) hoop

Mill Hill antique glass beads 3037 *(abalone)*

33 gauge white covered wire (detached pods):
*two 12 cm (4½ in) lengths (colour wires Pea Green
if desired, Copic YG63 Pea Green)*

33 gauge white covered wire (detached petal):
9 cm (3½ in) length

Stems

1. Work the pea pod stems in chain stitch with two strands of dark leaf-green thread in a size 9 crewel needle.

2. Work the pea flower stem in stem stitch with two strands of dark leaf-green thread.

Leaves

The leaves are embroidered with one strand of thread in a size 10 crewel needle.

1. Work the central vein in split stitch with dark pea-green thread.

2. Embroider each side of the leaf with long buttonhole stitches, using dark pea-green thread for one side, and medium leaf-green for the other. Work the buttonhole stitches at an angle, inserting the needle under the central vein to avoid a gap (the ridge of the buttonhole forms the leaf outline).

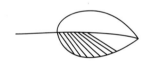

Pea Pods

The pea pods are embroidered with one strand of medium pea-green thread.

BACKGROUND PEA PODS

1. Work a row of stem stitch around the pea pod outlines on the background fabric.

2. Embroider each pea pod with consecutive rows of stem stitch, working all the rows from the top of the pod towards the pointed tip.

3. Using nylon thread, back stitch a row of beads (peas) to the surface of the embroidered pea pods, 1 mm away from the outer edges (the 'open sides') of the pea pods. Start the row of beads 5 mm (3/16 in) down from the top of the pod, and leave a space of 2–3 mm at the lower tip (8–9 beads).

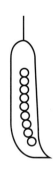

Detached Pea Pods

The pea pods are embroidered with one strand of medium pea-green thread.

1. Mount muslin into a small hoop and trace the detached pea pod outlines, aligning the straight edges of the pods with the straight grain of the fabric (check that the shapes have not been reversed—the left side pod is larger than the right).

2. Couch a 12 cm (4½ in) length of wire around the detached pea pod outline, leaving two wire tails at the top of the pod that touch but do not cross. Buttonhole-stitch the wire to the muslin.

3. Embroider the pea pod with consecutive rows of stem stitch, working all rows from the top of the pea pod towards the pointed tip. Carefully cut out the detached pea pods, as close to the stitched edge as possible.

To Complete the Pea Pods

1. Using a large yarn darner, apply the detached pea pod over the beaded background pod by inserting the wire tails at the end of the pea pod stem (check that the correct shape has been applied). Bend the wires behind the background pod and secure.

2. Carefully bend the sides of the detached pod over the beads to create a gentle curve. Using nylon thread in a size 12 sharps needle, secure the top of the detached pod over the background pod, with tiny stitches worked through the buttonholed edge (about 5 mm down from the stem). Position the detached pod so that the beads are just visible on the 'open' (outer) side, then secure the inner edges of the pod to the background fabric with tiny stitches worked in nylon thread.

3. Using one strand of dark pea-green thread in a size 12 sharps needle, work three detached chain stitches from the end of the stem into the top of the pod, to form the sepals.

*completed
pea pods*

Pea Flower

BACKGROUND PETALS

1. Outline the upper background petal in back stitch with one strand of magenta thread. Work a row of close, long and short buttonhole stitch around the curved lower edge of the petal, enclosing the outline. Embroider the remainder of the petal in long and short stitch.

2. Embroider the lower petal in the same way using light mauve thread.

DETACHED PETAL

1. Mount muslin into a small hoop and trace the detached pea flower petal outline. With one strand of medium mauve thread, couch wire around the lower curved edge of the petal outline, leaving a wire tail at each end of the upper 'fold' line. Buttonhole-stitch the wire to the muslin.

2. Using medium mauve thread, work a row of long and short buttonhole stitch around the lower edge of the petal (inside the wire), using the diagram as a guide to stitch direction. Embroider the remainder of the petal in long and short stitch working up to the 'fold' line.

3. Cut out the petal close to the wire edge, leaving a small turning (2 mm/⅛1/8 in) at the 'fold' edge. Finger-press the turning under.

TO COMPLETE THE PEA FLOWER

1. Using a fine yarn darner, apply the detached petal over the embroidered background petals, inserting one wire tail at the end of the stem and the other at the outer edge. Bend wires behind the flower and hold with tape—secure and trim when the flower is complete. Tuck the fold under and slip stitch the edge to the background fabric, just above the top edge of the background petals (or lift the petal up and carefully stitch along the fold). Shape the detached petal over the background petals with tweezers.

2. To embroider the sepals, work three detached chain stitches, from the end of the stem into the base of the flower, with one strand of medium pea-green thread.

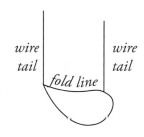

wire tail   *wire tail*
fold line

stitch direction guidelines

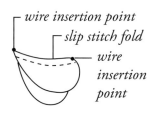

wire insertion point
slip stitch fold
wire insertion point

completed pea flower

Ladybird

Requirements

black stranded thread: *DMC 310*

red stranded thread: *DMC 349*

black metallic thread: *Kreinik Cord 005c*

red cotton fabric (homespun):
15 cm (6 in) square

Mill Hill petite beads 42014 *(black)*

33 gauge white covered wire (ladybird):
10 cm (4 in) length (colour red if desired in Copic R17 Lipstick Orange)

not actual size

Abdomen

With one strand of black thread, outline the abdomen with small back stitches, then embroider with padded satin stitch, working the stitches across the shape.

Detached Wings

1. Mount red cotton fabric into a small hoop and trace the wing outline, placing the straight inner edges of the wings on the straight grain of the fabric.

2. Fold the wire in half to form a ∧ shape. With one strand of red thread, couch the wire around the wing outlines, making the first stitch at the top of the **Λ** inside the wings, and leaving two tails of wire at the top that touch but do not cross. Overcast stitch the wire to the fabric then work a row of split stitch inside the wire.

3. Embroider the wings in padded satin stitch, working the satin stitches parallel to the straight inner edge of the wings.

4. With one strand of black thread, embroider a spot on each wing in satin stitch, working 2–3 stitches *across* the red satin stitches.

To Complete the Ladybird

1. Cut out the wings and shape with tweezers, pushing the straight inner edges together and curving the wings into a rounded shape. Using a yarn darner, insert the wire tails through • at the top edge of the abdomen. Bend the wires towards the tail of the ladybird and secure at the back of the abdomen with a few stitches. For extra security (especially for tiny ladybirds), bend the wires back towards the head and stitch again. Trim wire.

2. With one strand of black thread in a sharps needle, work wide satin stitches over the wire insertion point to form the head of the ladybird. Apply two petite black beads for eyes.

3. Using one strand of black metallic thread in a size 9 milliners needle, work two straight stitches for each leg. Work two straight stitches for the antennae. Gently shape the wings with tweezers.

Crab Apple

The Crab Apple, *Malus sylvestris* ('forest apple'), is a small, hardy, deciduous tree with lightly scented blossoms ranging in colour from white, through shades of pink to magenta. Often found in hedgerows, the trees bear small, hard fruit which is traditionally made into jellies, preserves and wine.

The delicately flavoured, rosy-red fruit of the crab apple was known as 'crab' by country people in Shakespeare's time. 'Crabs' roasted before the fire and put into ale were a favourite treat, especially in the wassail-bowl at Christmas, and are referred to in the 'Song of Winter' in *Love's Labour's Lost*:

> *When roasted crabs hiss in the bowl*
> *Then nightly sings the staring owl.*
> LOVE'S LABOUR'S LOST (v.2)

This beverage, consisting of ale, nutmeg, sugar, toast and roasted crabs, was called Lambs-wool, and is still served at one of the colleges at Cambridge University. Lambs-wool was also popular at christenings. The godparents were sometimes called 'gossips', and the christening mug was known as 'the gossip's bowl'—the bowl alluded to in *A Midsummer Night's Dream* where Puck, disguised by magic as a crab apple, says:

> *And sometime lurk I in a gossip's bowl,*
> *In very likeness of a roasted crab,*
> *And when she drinks, against her lips I bob*
> *And on her wither'd dewlap pour the ale.*
> A MIDSUMMER NIGHT'S DREAM (ii.1)

162

CRAB APPLE : METHOD

Requirements

medium pink stranded thread:
Soie d'Alger 1012 or DMC 761

light pink stranded thread:
Soie d'Alger 1011 or DMC 3713

very pale pink stranded thread:
Soie d'Alger 3041 or DMC 819

dark coral stranded thread:
Soie d'Alger 2915 or DMC 3712

medium coral stranded thread:
Soie d'Alger 2914 or DMC 760

dark yellow stranded thread:
Soie d'Alger 545 or DMC 742

lime-green stranded thread:
Soie d'Alger 2143 or DMC 166

dark leaf-green stranded thread:
Soie d'Alger 2126 or DMC 937

medium leaf-green stranded thread:
Soie d'Alger 2125 or DMC 469

light leaf-green stranded thread:
Soie d'Alger 2124 or DMC 470

ecru stranded thread: *DMC Ecru*

quilter's muslin:
*20 cm (8 in) square in a 13 cm
(5 in) hoop*

not actual size

white felt: *5 x 8 cm (2 x 3 in)*

paper-backed fusible web:
5 x 8 cm (2 x 3 in)

33 gauge white covered wire (detached
petals):
seven 9 cm (3½ in) lengths

Stems

Work the stems for the leaf and the buds in stem stitch with two strands of dark leaf-green thread in a size 9 crewel needle.

Leaf

The leaf is embroidered with one strand of thread in a size 10 crewel needle.

1. Work the central vein in split stitch with medium leaf-green thread.

2. Embroider each side of the lower leaf with long buttonhole stitches, using medium leaf-green thread for one side, and light leaf-green for the other. Work both side of the upper leaf in light leaf-green thread. Work the buttonhole stitches at an angle, inserting the needle under the central vein to avoid a gap.

completed stems & leaf

Buds

The crab apple buds are worked on quilter's muslin as detached, wired shapes, using one strand of thread in a size 10 crewel needle. The buds and the detached crab apple petals may be worked on one piece of muslin.

1. Mount a square of muslin into a 13 cm (5 in) hoop and trace the two detached bud outlines. Five detached petals will also be worked on this hoop of muslin.

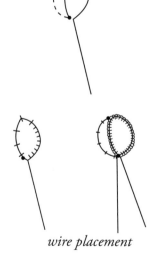

wire placement

2. Cut a length of wire in two. Using dark coral thread, couch one wire around the main segment of the bud outline, starting with an end of wire at the centre • , and bending the tail of wire at the base (next to the centre •) as shown. Buttonhole stitch the wire to the muslin.

3. Couch the second wire around the remainder of the bud outline, starting with an end of wire at the upper • (next to the buttonhole edge), and bending the tail of wire at the base as shown. Buttonhole stitch the wire to the muslin.

4. Using dark coral thread, work a row of long and short buttonhole stitch around the top edge of the bud shape (working on either side of the centre line). Embroider the rest of the bud in long and short stitch with medium coral thread, working all stitches towards the base of the bud. Repeat for the second bud (the shape is reversed). Carefully cut out the shapes, close to the buttonholed edge, avoiding the wire tails.

To Complete the Buds

The detached bud shapes are applied to the background over a padding of felt.

1. Trace two sets of bud padding shapes to the paper-backed fusible web then fuse to the white felt. Cut out the shapes.

felt padding

2. With one strand of medium coral thread, apply the felt padding to the background, inside the bud outline, with small stab stitches around the outside edges, applying the smaller shape first.

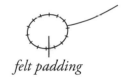

felt padding

3. Using a yarn darner, insert the detached bud wire tails at the end of the bud stem, bending the wires behind the felt padding. Hold the tails with masking tape. Gently shape the bud over the padding then, using dark coral thread in a size 12 sharps needle, attach the outside edge of the bud by working invisible stitches into the buttonholed edge. Secure the wires with small stitches. Trim tails.

— small stab stitches

4. Using light leaf-green thread, work three chain stitches into the base of the bud to form the sepals. With medium leaf-green thread, work some straight stitches at the end of the bud stem to form a base.

completed buds

Flower

The five detached crab apple flower petals are worked with three shades of pale pink, using one strand of thread in a size 10 crewel needle. To avoid soiling the pale edges of the petals with a traced lead pencil outline, the wires are bent into a petal shape first, before applying to the muslin. Use tweezers, and the detached crab apple petal outline as a template, to bend the wires into the required petal shapes.

On a square of muslin mounted into a 13 cm (5 in) hoop, work five detached petals, using the shades of pink as follows:

PETALS 1 & 2

1. Shape a 9 cm (3½ in) length of wire around the detached petal outline, leaving two tails of wire at the base that touch but do not cross. Using medium pink thread, couch the shaped wire to the muslin, then stitch with small, close buttonhole stitches, incorporating the couching stitches.

2. With light pink thread, work a row of long and short buttonhole stitch inside the top edge of the petal (close to the wire). Embroider the rest of the petal in long and short stitch with very pale pink thread, working all stitches towards the base of the petal.

PETALS 3 & 4

1. Shape a length of wire around the detached petal outline. Using light pink thread, couch then buttonhole stitch the shaped wire to the muslin.

2. Work a row of long and short buttonhole stitch inside the top edge of the petal with light pink thread. Embroider the rest of the petal in long and short stitch with very pale pink thread.

PETAL 5

1. Shape a length of wire around the detached petal outline. Using light pink thread, couch then buttonhole stitch the shaped wire to the muslin.

2. Using very pale pink thread, work a row of long and short buttonhole stitch inside the top edge of the petal then embroider the rest of the petal in long and short stitch.

TO COMPLETE THE FLOWER

1. Carefully cut out the petals, close to the buttonholed edge, avoiding the wire tails.

2. Make five evenly spaced pencil dots around the small circle outline. Using a yarn darner, insert the wire tails of the detached petals, selected as desired, through the five dots. Bend the wires behind the petals and secure to the backing fabric with small stitches using ecru thread. Do not cut the wires until the flower is finished. Shape the petals with tweezers.

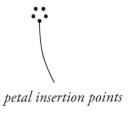

petal insertion points

3. Work the centre of the crab apple with French knots, using two strands of either lime green or dark yellow thread in a size 9 milliners needle. Using lime green thread, fill the centre of the flower with French knots. With dark yellow thread, work a few knots in the centre and some into the base of the petals. Trim the wires.

completed flower

Bee

not actual size

Requirements

old gold stranded thread: *DMC 783*

black stranded thread: *DMC 310*

gold/black metallic thread:
Kreinik Cord 205c

gold rayon machine thread:
Madeira Rayon 1055

nylon clear thread:
Madeira Monofil 60 col. 1001

ecru stranded thread:
DMC Ecru

honey mottled organza:
15 cm (6 in) square

pearl metal organdie:
15 cm (6 in) square

Mill Hill Glass Beads 374 *(oilslick)*

28 gauge silver uncovered wire (wings):
three 10 cm (4 in) lengths

Thorax & Abdomen

1. Outline the abdomen and the small circle next to it (the thorax) with small back stitches using one strand of black thread.

2. The abdomen is filled with consecutive rows of Turkey knots, worked with two strands of either old gold or black thread in a size 9 crewel needle. Starting at the 'thorax end' of the abdomen, work two rows of Turkey knots in black, then two rows in old gold thread. Work two more rows in black, two rows in old gold, then two rows in black at the tail (adjust the number of rows for each stripe, if necessary, to end up with a black tail). The Turkey knots should pierce the back stitches but not protrude outside them.

3. Cut the loops between the Turkey knots and comb the threads upwards. Carefully cut and comb the threads to form a velvety mound for the abdomen.

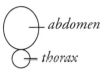

abdomen
thorax

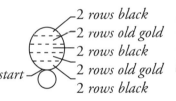

2 rows black
2 rows old gold
2 rows black
2 rows old gold
2 rows black
start

Wings

1. Mount the honey mottled organza and the pearl metal organdie (as a backing) into a small hoop, one layer of fabric rotated 45 degrees to be on the bias grain (the wing fabrics are not fused together).

2. Bend silver wire around the wing outline templates—two fore wings and two hind wings—leaving two tails of wire at the base of the wing that touch but do not cross. Place the wire shapes on the hoop of wing fabric—holding the wire tails in place with masking tape. Make sure that you have a right and a left fore wing and a right and a left hind wing.

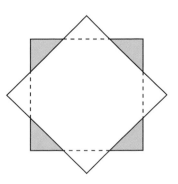

3. Using one strand of gold rayon machine thread in a sharps needle, stitch the wire to the wing fabric with small, close, overcast stitches, working several stitches over both wires, at the base of the wing, to begin and end the stitching.

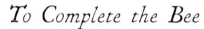

4. With one strand of gold/black metallic thread in a size 9 milliners needle, work a fly stitch in each wing for veins, retaining the tails of thread at the corners of the wings. Carefully cut out the wings, taking care not to cut the tails of metallic thread.

To Complete the Bee

1. Using a large yarn darner, insert the wings through two separate holes, inside the stitched thorax outline—the right fore and hind wings together through one hole and the left fore and hind wings through the other (they will be very close together). Bend the wires to the sides (under the wings) and stitch to the backing with tiny stitches using ecru thread. Do not trim the wire tails until the bee is finished.

2. Using two strands of black thread, work Turkey knots between the wings to fill the thorax (approximately eight knots). Cut and comb the Turkey knots to form a velvety mound.

3. To form the head/eyes, stitch two oilslick seed beads (side by side with one stitch), very close to the thorax, using one strand of black thread. Work another stitch through both beads then a stitch between the beads (across the previous stitches towards the thorax). Push the beads together with tweezers.

4. With two strands of gold/black metallic thread in a milliners needle, stitch six legs, working three back stitches for each leg. Work a fly stitch for the antennae with one strand of metallic thread.

Caterpillar

Requirements

russet stranded thread: *DMC 920*

dark blue stranded thread: *DMC 791*

Mill Hill Glass Beads 374 *(oilslick)*

not actual size

The caterpillar has thirteen segments plus a head. On the skeleton outline, the caterpillar body is indicated by twelve straight lines and a dot at each end. The caterpillar is worked in raised stem stitch over padding.

1. With six strands of russet thread in a chenille needle, work four long stitches between the two dots to pad the caterpillar. With one strand of russet thread, work twelve couching stitches over the padding, using the lines from the skeleton outline as a guide.

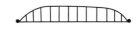

2. Using russet thread, stitch an oilslick seed bead at the upper end of the padding for the head, the hole in the bead parallel to the stem. Work approximately eight rows of raised stem stitch, over the couching stitches, to fill the caterpillar, taking about four rows through the head bead.

3. Each segment has a russet spike at the top. With one strand of russet thread in a size 12 sharps needle, work a tiny straight stitch into each segment, including one above the head.

4. Work two tiny French knots in each of twelve segments using dark blue thread in a size 10 crewel needle.

Primrose

Primrose, first-born child of Ver,
Merry spring-time's harbinger.

The Two Noble Kinsmen (i.1)

The Primrose, *Primula vulgaris*, was welcomed as one of the earliest spring flowers, the name deriving from the Old French *primerose* or Latin *prima rosa*, 'first flower'.

Although found in varying shades of yellow and green, in literature the Primrose seems usually to be denoted as 'faint' and 'pale', perhaps referencing their meaning of 'early youth' or 'sadness' in the language of flowers. In *A Winter's Tale*, Shakespeare referred to them as 'pale primroses that die unmarried'.

In the early days of medicine, the Primrose was considered an important remedy for muscular rheumatism, paralysis and gout. An infusion of flowers was considered excellent against nervous hysterical disorders, and 'Primrose tea', claimed Gerard, 'drunk in the month of May, is famous for curing the phrensie':

A practitioner of London who was famous for curing the phrensie, after he had performed his cure by the due observation of physick, accustomed every yeare in the moneth of May to dyet his Patients after this manner: Take the

leaves and floures of Primrose, boile them a little in fountaine water, and in some rose and Betony waters, adding thereto sugar, pepper, salt, and butter, which being strained, he gave them to drinke thereof first and last.

John Gerard, *THE HERBALL* (1597)

Primrose border from Miss Higgin's Handbook of Embroidery *(1912)*

The primrose has always been a favourite flower, yet it seems to have often been associated with sadness, and a more negative connotation—that of the 'primrose path', a term which was coined by Shakespeare to refer to a life of ease and pleasure, or to a course of action that seems easy and appropriate, but can actually end in calamity. Thus, in *Hamlet*, Ophelia warns her brother, Laertes, to refrain from lecturing her on how to behave, while ignoring his own advice:

... But, my good brother,
Do not, as some ungracious pastors do,
Show me the steep and thorny way to heaven;
Whiles, like a puff'd and reckless libertine,
Himself the primrose path of dalliance treads,
And recks not his own rede.

HAMLET (i.3)

not actual size

Requirements

dark yellow stranded thread:
Soie d'Alger 545 or DMC 742

medium yellow stranded thread:
Soie d'Alger 542 or DMC 744

dark leaf-green stranded thread:
Soie d'Alger 2126 or DMC 937

medium leaf-green stranded thread:
Soie d'Alger 2125 or DMC 469

light leaf-green stranded thread:
Soie d'Alger 2124 or DMC 470

nylon clear thread:
Madeira Monofil 60 col. 1001

ecru stranded thread: *DMC Ecru*

quilter's muslin:
20 cm (8 in) square in a 13 cm (5 in) hoop

Mill Hill frosted glass beads 62049 *(green)*

33 gauge white covered wire (detached petals):
seven 9 cm (3½ in) lengths

Stems

Work the bud stem in stem stitch with two strands of dark leaf-green thread in a size 9 crewel needle.

Leaf

The leaves are worked with one strand of thread in a size 10 crewel needle.

1. Work the central vein in split stitch with dark leaf-green thread.

2. Outline the leaves with stem stitch, then fill with consecutive rows of stem stitch, working one side in medium leaf-green thread and the other side in light leaf-green. Work each row in the same direction, staggering the ends of the rows as required to fill the shape.

*completed
stems & leaves*

Flower & Bud

The primrose flower and bud require seven detached petals, all worked with one strand of thread in a size 10 crewel needle.

Mount a square of muslin into a 13 cm (5 in) hoop and trace five detached flower petal outlines and two detached bud petal outlines.

FLOWER & BUD PETALS

1. Using medium yellow thread, couch wire around the petal outline, leaving two tails at the base. Buttonhole stitch the wire to the muslin.

2. Work a row of long and short buttonhole stitch inside the top edge of the petal (close to the wire), then embroider the petal in long and short stitch, working all stitches towards the base of the petal.

3. Work a green and yellow marking at the base of each flower petal (the bud petals do not have this marking). Using light leaf-green thread, make a stitch from the base of the petal into the petal surface (about 3 mm long). With dark yellow thread, work four straight stitches on either side of the central green stitch. Carefully cut out the petals.

TO COMPLETE THE FLOWER

1. Make five evenly spaced pencil dots around the centre circle outline. Using a yarn darner, insert the wire tails of the five detached petals through the five dots. Bend the wires behind the petals and secure to the backing fabric using ecru thread. Do not cut the wires until the flower is finished.

2. Using nylon thread, stitch a green bead in the centre of the primrose, the hole in the bead facing upwards.

completed flower

3. Shape the petals with tweezers, pushing them gently towards the centre. With one strand of light leaf-green thread in a size 12 needle, make another green stitch into the centre of each petal, working from the base of the petal (next to the bead) and piercing the previous green stitch. Trim the wires.

To Complete the Bud

1. Using medium yellow thread, work the background bud petals with long buttonhole stitches, the ridge of the stitch forming the top edge of the petals.

2. With medium leaf-green thread, outline the bud base with small back stitches. Work three chain stitches, inside the outline, to pad the base. Embroider the base in satin stitch, enclosing the outline.

3. Using a yarn darner, insert the wire tails of the detached petals through two holes at the top of the base (at the base of the background petals): one petal will overlap the other. Secure the wires behind the base and trim.

completed bud

4. With one strand of light leaf-green thread, work three detached chain stitches from the top of the base into the petals to form the sepals.

Honeysuckle

Sleep thou, and I will wind thee in my arms.
So doth the woodbine the sweet honeysuckle
Gently entwist; the female ivy so
Enrings the barky fingers of the elm.

A Midsummer Night's Dream (iv.1)

The Honeysuckle, *Lonicera periclymenum,* is the emblem of affection and faithfulness. With its twining stems, rich creamy yellow flowers and pretty red fruit, it is one of the loveliest plants of the hedgerow. A true plant of midsummer, the flowers open when warmed by the sun, and give off a strong honey-sweet scent. The name *Lonicera* was given to it by Linnaeus in honour of Adam Lonicer, a sixteenth-century naturalist.

Honeysuckle embroidery motifs: (right, John Overton; left, Richard Shorleyker)

Honeysuckle was also known as Woodbine or Woodbind, from its habit of twining its stems around any tree or bush near to it, keeping its hold so tight as to leave its mark in deep grooves on the wood that has supported it. These tough fibrous stems were used to bind brooms and for textiles.

The name Woodbine has often been used to describe any creeping or climbing plant, however, Shakespeare used both names to describe the same plant—Woodbine referred to the twisting nature of the plant generally, and Honeysuckle to the flower—as seen in *A Midsummer Night's Dream* when Queen Titania whispers to poor bewitched Nick Bottom.

Honeysuckle was popular in Elizabethan gardens, both for its fragrance and as a shade for covered walks and bowers. As it grew thickly, it also provided both shelter and a hiding place for lovers and secret trysts—in *Much Ado about Nothing*, Hero bids her cousin, Beatrice:

... steal into the pleached bower
Where honeysuckles, ripen'd by the sun,
Forbid the sun to enter.
   MUCH ADO ABOUT NOTHING (iii.1)

not actual size

Requirements

dark orange stranded thread:
Soie d'Alger 913 or DMC 350

light orange stranded thread:
Soie d'Alger 643 or DMC 3825

pale yellow stranded thread:
Soie d'Alger 621 or DMC 3855

dark yellow stranded thread:
Soie d'Alger 545 or DMC 742

lime-green stranded thread:
Soie d'Alger 2143 or DMC 166

dark leaf-green stranded thread:
Soie d'Alger 2126 or DMC 937

medium leaf-green stranded thread:
Soie d'Alger 2125 or DMC 469

ecru stranded thread: *DMC Ecru*

nylon clear thread:
Madeira Monofil 60 col. 1001

quilter's muslin:
20 cm (8 in) square in a 15 cm (6in) hoop

2.5 mm gold bead

33 gauge white covered wire (detached petals):
three 13 cm (5 in) lengths

Stems

Work the leaf stems in stem stitch with two strands of dark leaf-green thread in a size 9 crewel needle.

Leaf

The leaves are worked with one strand of thread in a size 10 crewel needle.

1. Work the central vein in split stitch with dark leaf-green thread.

2. Embroider each side of the leaf with long buttonhole stitches, using medium leaf-green thread. Work the buttonhole stitches at an angle, inserting the needle under the central vein to avoid a gap.

Flower

The honeysuckle flower is worked with one strand of thread in a size 10 crewel needle.

*completed
stems & leaves*

BACKGROUND PETALS

Using dark orange thread, outline the petals with small back stitches then work chain stitches, inside the outline, as padding. Embroider each petal in satin stitch, working the stitches at an angle and enclosing the outline.

DETACHED PETALS

As the outer edge of the honeysuckle petal curves back over the narrower inner section, the detached petals are worked on both sides of the fabric in the hoop.

1. Mount a square of muslin into a 13 or 12 cm (6 or 5 in) hoop (a larger hoop facilitates the working of these petals). Trace three detached honeysuckle petal outlines, aligning the straight edges of the petals with the straight grain of the fabric.

2. Using tweezers, shape a length of wire around the detached honeysuckle petal outline diagram, leaving two tails at the base of the petal. The wire tails will be inserted through the muslin at the wire insertion points on the traced petal outline. The curved outer edge of the petal will be worked on the upper side of the fabric, and the lower narrower section of the petal will be worked on the back of the fabric.

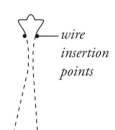

wire insertion points

3. Insert the wire tails through the wire insertion points, leaving the curved outer end of the petal on the upper surface of the fabric (hold the tails of wire at the back with masking tape). Using pale yellow thread, couch the shaped wire around the outer petal outline, between the wire insertion points, then buttonhole-stitch the wire to the muslin. Work a row of long and short buttonhole stitch inside the top edge of the petal (close to the wire), then embroider the outer end of the petal (up to the wire insertion points) with long and short stitch.

4. Turn the hoop over—the narrower, lower end of the petal will be worked on the back of the fabric. With light orange thread, and using the traced outline on the front as a guide, couch the wires along the straight lower sides of the petal, leaving two wire tails at the base of the petal that touch but do not cross. Buttonhole-stitch the wires to the muslin. Embroider the narrow space between the wires with long and short stitch, working up to the pale yellow section. Turn the hoop over, then work five straight stitches over the base of yellow embroidered area of the petal with the light orange thread. Carefully cut the petals out. To shape the petals, gently squeeze the lower sides of the petal to look like a narrow tube, then turn the pale yellow outer edge of the petal back over the lower petal.

To Complete the Flower

1. Make three pencil dots on the centre circle, between the background petals as shown.

2. Using a yarn darner, insert the wire tails of the detached petals through the three dots. Bend the wires behind the petals and secure to the backing fabric with small stitches using ecru thread. Do not cut the wires until the flower is finished. Adjust the position of the petals then secure invisibly to the background by carefully lifting up the yellow section and working a few tiny stitches with nylon thread in a size 12 sharps needle. Bend the outer edge of the petal back and shape with tweezers. Using one strand of lime thread, work a straight stitch (5 mm) from the wire insertion point into the base of each petal.

3. Work five stamens at the end of each petal—each stamen consists of a straight stitch with a French knot at the end. Work the centre stamen in lime green, then two stamens on either side in dark yellow.

4. Using nylon thread, stitch a gold bead in the centre of the honeysuckle.

completed flower

LANCASTER Rose

And here I prophesy; this brawl to-day
Grown to this faction in the Temple garden,
Shall send, between the red rose and the white,
A thousand souls to death and deadly night.

Henry VI, Part 1 (ii.4)

Rose embroidery motif (John Overton)

The classic red rose, *Rosa gallica officinalis*, which originally grew wild in southern Europe, is thought to be the oldest cultivated rose. In the thirteenth century, a cultivated form of *Rosa gallica* was brought from Damascus by Thibault, the troubadour Count of Champagne, and established in the gardens of Provins, southern France. *Rosa gallica officinalis* is also known as the Rose of Provins, the French or Gallic Rose, the Apothecary Rose and the Red Rose of Lancaster.

There is no flower so often mentioned by Shakespeare as the rose—be it the Red Rose, the White Rose, the Musk Rose, the Provencal Rose, the Damask

Left: Rose design from
The Craftsman's Plant Book
by Ralph Hatton (1909)
Below: a painted engraving
of a Rosa Gallica *by*
Pierre-Joseph Redoute

Rose, the Variegated Rose, the Canker Rose (the wild Dog Rose), or the Sweet Briar. He, along with Gerard, would probably have considered it to be the queen of flowers:

The Rose doth deserve the chief and prime place among all floures whatsoever; being not onely esteemed for his beauty, vertues, and his fragrant and odoriferous smell; but also because it is the honor and ornament of our English Scepter, as by the conjunction appeareth, in the uniting of those two most Royall Houses of Lancaster and Yorke.

John Gerard, *THE HERBALL* (1597)

The red rose, *Rosa gallica officinalis,* became the symbol of the House of Lancaster in the Wars of the Roses. Upon Henry Tudor's ascension to the throne the Red Rose of Lancaster was merged with the White Rose of York to form the Tudor Rose—the plant emblem of England. Shakespeare references the red and white roses of the Houses of York and Lancaster in many passages, including the scene in *Henry VI, Part 1*, that is traditionally supposed to have started the Wars of the Roses.

PLANTAGENET: *Let him that is a true-born gentleman*
And stands upon the honour of his birth,
If he suppose that I have pleaded truth,
From off this brier pluck a white rose with me.

SOMERSET: *Let him that is no coward nor no flatterer,*
But dare maintain the party of the truth,
Pluck a red rose from off this thorn with me.

The prophetic words of the Earl of Warwick follow:

And here I prophesy; this brawl to-day
Grown to this faction in the Temple garden,
Shall send, between the red rose and the white,
A thousand souls to death and deadly night.
HENRY *VI*, PART *1* (ii.4)

Forms of heraldic
Tudor Rose

It appears that in Shakespeare's time, one of the fashions of the day was the wearing of enormous 'roses' on the shoes. When *Hamlet* (iii.2) speaks of wearing 'two Provincial roses on my razed shoes', he is not referring to a fresh rose picked in the garden, but to the rosettes made of silk ribbon in the shape of roses of Provins, which were much worn by the gentlemen at the court of Queen Elizabeth ('razed' meaning slashed, inlaid with different coloured silks, stitched and perhaps embroidered). This quote from Friar Bacon's *Prophecy* (1604) also alludes to this fashion:

When roses in the gardens grew,
And not in ribbons on a shoe:
Now ribbon roses take such place
That garden roses want their grace.

Probably one of the finest embroidered book covers in existence, this bible was
presented by the printer, Christopher Barker, to Queen Elizabeth on New Year's Day, 1584.
Bound in crimson velvet, it was described at the time as *'covered with crymson vellat alouer
embradered wythe venys golde and seade perle'*. The design consists of a scroll of six rose stems,
bearing flowers, buds, and leaves springing from a large central rose, with four auxiliary
scrolls crossing the corners and intertwining at their ends. The large rose in the centre, and
those near the corners are all Tudor roses. *43 x 30 cm (17 x 12 in).*

not actual size

Requirements

dark red stranded thread:
Soie d'Alger 1016 or DMC 304

medium red stranded thread:
Soie d'Alger 1015 or DMC 321

medium yellow stranded thread:
Soie d'Alger 542 or DMC 744

dark leaf-green stranded thread:
Soie d'Alger 2126 or DMC 937

dark pea-green stranded thread:
Soie d'Alger 1834 or DMC 367

quilter's muslin:
20 cm (8 in) square in a 10 cm (4 in) hoop

Mill Hill Frosted Glass Beads 62049 *(green)*

33 gauge white covered wire (detached rose petals):
*five 9 cm (3½ in) lengths (colour wires red if desired,
Copic R17 (Lipstick Orange)*

Stems

Work the leaf and bud stem in stem stitch with two strands of dark leaf-green thread in a size 9 crewel needle.

Leaf

The leaves are worked with one strand of thread in a size 10 crewel needle.

1. Work the central vein in split stitch with dark leaf-green thread.

2. Embroider each side of the leaf with long buttonhole stitches, using dark leaf-green thread for one side, and dark pea-green for the other. Work the buttonhole stitches at an angle, inserting the needle under the central vein to avoid a gap.

completed leaf

Bud

The rose bud is worked with one strand of thread in a size 10 crewel needle.

1. Using medium red thread, work the rose bud petals with long buttonhole stitches, the ridge of the stitch forming the top edge of the petals.

2. Using dark leaf-green thread, outline the bud base with small back stitches. Work three chain stitches, inside the outline, to pad the base. Embroider the base in satin stitch, working from the stem end into the base of the petals and enclosing the outline.

completed bud

3. The sepals are worked with detached chain stitches using one strand of dark pea-green thread. Work three chain stitches from the top of the base over the petals. Make the tie-down stitch slightly elongated to give a pointed end to the sepal.

Flower

The rose is worked with one strand of thread in a size 10 crewel needle.

BACKGROUND PETALS

1. Using medium red thread, outline the petals in long and short buttonhole stitch. Work the stitches close together, keeping the stitch direction towards the centre of the rose. Embroider the rest of the petals with long and short stitch.

2. To form the sepals, work two detached chain stitches (one inside the other) between each petal, using dark pea-green thread.

DETACHED PETALS

1. Mount a square of muslin into a 10 cm (4 in) hoop and trace five detached rose petal outlines.

2. Using medium red thread, couch wire around the petal outline, leaving two tails at the base. Buttonhole stitch the wire to the muslin.

3. Work a row of long and short buttonhole stitch inside the top edge of the petal (close to the wire), using medium red thread for two of the petals, and dark red thread for the remaining three petals.

4. Using dark red thread, fill the petals with long and short stitch, blending into the long and short buttonhole stitches and working all stitches towards the base of the petal. Carefully cut out the petals.

To Complete the Flower

1. Make five evenly spaced pencil dots around the centre circle outline, offsetting them in relation to the background petals as shown.

2. Using a yarn darner, insert the wire tails of one petal through two separate dots. Bend the wires behind the petals and secure. Repeat for each of the petals (adjacent petals will share insertion points—the side edges of the petals will overlap). Do not cut the wires until the flower is finished.

3. With two strands of medium yellow thread in a size 9 milliners needle, work a circle of ten Turkey knots inside the circle outline—two knots at the base of each petal—leaving a small space in the centre. Keep the tails of the Turkey knots quite long (5 cm/2 in) to make the centre easier to manage (the knots are really close together).

4. With one strand of medium yellow thread, stitch a green bead, on its side, in the centre of the space. Work two stitches through the bead, taking care not to catch the Turkey knots (the hole in the bead is not visible).

5. Cut the loops of the Turkey knots then comb the threads into a bundle (like a tassel) above the surface of the petals. Holding the bundle firmly, cut straight across the threads, just above the bead (about 5 mm above the surface of the fabric). Take care to hold the blades of the scissors parallel to the background. Shape the petals then trim the wires.

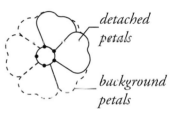

detached petals insertion points

detached petals

background petals

completed flower

Bluebell

Thou shalt not lack
The flower that's like thy face, pale primrose, nor
The azured harebell, like thy veins.

Cymbeline (iv.2)

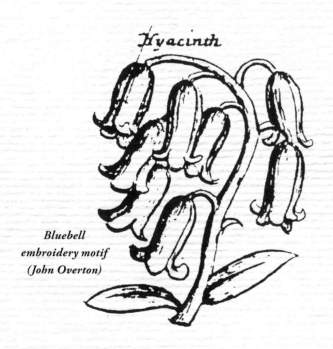

Bluebell
embroidery motif
(John Overton)

Although he uses the name 'harebell' in *Cymbeline*, Shakespeare was almost certainly referring to the wild hyacinth, or bluebell, when he wrote of its 'azured' blue.

One of the most loved and colourful of English wildflowers, the Bluebell, *Hyacinthoides non-scripta*, forms sweetly-scented carpets of misty green and blue throughout ancient woodland in spring. Common names for the Bluebell include British Bluebell, Wild Hyacinth, Wood Bell,

Fairy Flower And Bellbottle, while in Scotland, the term 'bluebell' refers to the much paler blue harebell (*Campanula rotundifolia*).

The slender curved stems of the Bluebell, which can reach up to 50 cm (20 in) in height, bear 5–12 deep violet-blue flowers, each shaped like a narrow straight-sided bell which curls up at the end.

The stem and bulb of the Bluebell contains a sticky juice which could be used as a starch for the ruffs worn around the neck and cuffs of garments in Elizabethan times. It was also used as a bookbinder's gum, and even for adhering feathers to arrows.

The blew Hare-bells or English Jacinth is very common throughout all England. It hath long narrow leaves leaning towards the ground, among the which spring up naked or bare stalks loden with many hollow blew floures, of a strong sweet smell ... The root is bulbous, full of a slimie glewish juice, which will serve to set feathers upon arrowes in stead of glew, or to paste bookes with: hereof is made the best starch next unto that of Wake-robin roots.

John Gerard, THE HERBALL (1597)

not actual size

Requirements

dark blue stranded thread:
Soie d'Alger 4916 or DMC 791

medium blue stranded thread:
Soie d'Alger 4914 or DMC 158

dark yellow stranded thread:
Soie d'Alger 545 or DMC 742

dark leaf-green stranded thread:
Soie d'Alger 2126 or DMC 937

dark pea-green stranded thread:
Soie d'Alger 1834 or DMC 367

quilter's muslin:
20 cm (8 in) square in a 13 cm (5 in) hoop

33 gauge white covered wire (detached bluebells):
two 9 cm (3½ in) lengths (colour wires blue if desired, Copic BV08 Blue Violet)

Stems

1. Work the bluebell stems in chain stitch with two strands of dark leaf-green thread in a size 9 crewel needle.

2. Work the leaf stem in stem stitch with two strands of dark leaf-green thread.

Leaf

The leaf is embroidered with one strand of thread in a size 10 crewel needle.

1. Work the central vein in split stitch with dark pea-green thread.

2. Embroider each side of the leaf with long buttonhole stitches, using dark pea-green thread. Work the buttonhole stitches at an angle, inserting the needle under the central vein to avoid a gap.

completed
leaf

Flowers

The bluebell flowers are worked with one strand of thread in a size 10 crewel needle.

BACKGROUND PETALS

1. Work a row of long and short buttonhole stitch along the lower edge of the bluebell with dark blue thread.

2. Using medium blue thread, work an outline around the bluebell in split stitch, then embroider the shape with long and short stitch, blending the medium blue into the dark blue at the lower edge.

DETACHED UPPER PETALS

1. Mount a square of muslin into a 13 cm (5 in) hoop and trace two upper bluebell petal outlines, aligning the side edges of the shapes with the straight grain of the fabric.

2. Using dark blue thread, couch, then buttonhole stitch a length of wire to the muslin along the lower edge of the bluebell, leaving a tail of wire at each end. Work a row of long and short buttonhole stitch along the lower edge of the bluebell, close to the wire. Stitch the inside petal lines in split stitch, working from the lower edge towards the top of the bluebell.

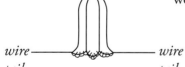

wire ————————— wire

3. With medium blue thread, outline the shape in split stitch then embroider the bluebell with long and short stitch, blending into the dark blue at the lower edge and working the stitches within the petal lines.

To Complete the Bluebell

The detached upper bluebell shapes are applied to the background over the embroidered petals.

1. Make a row of running stitches 1 mm away from the sides and top of the embroidered upper bluebell shape, leaving thread tails at each side. Carefully cut out the shape, leaving a small turning around the side and top edges and cutting close to the wire along the lower edge (taking care not to cut off the wire or thread tails).

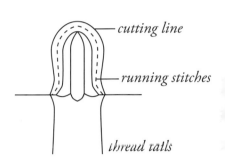

cutting line

running stitches

thread tails

2. To apply the upper bluebell shape, gently pull the thread tails and finger press the turning to the inside. Using a yarn darner, insert the wire tails though the lower corners of the background bluebell, crossing the wires behind the shape and holding with masking tape. Using medium blue thread, stab stitch the side and upper edges of the bluebell in place, positioning the top of the shape at the end of the bluebell stem. Work the stab stitches from the edge of the background shape into the edges of the applied shape, gently pulling the tails of the gathering thread to ease the shape to size (cut these away when no longer required). The blunt end of a yarn darner, held inside the shape, can be used to nudge the edge into position. A little stuffing, or thread scraps, may be inserted inside the bluebell to maintain the shape if required. Secure wires and trim.

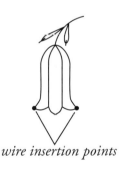

wire insertion points

3. With one strand of dark blue thread, work two chain stitches into the bluebell stem above the bluebells.

4. Using dark yellow thread, work three stamens inside the lower opening of each bluebell. Work a straight stitch with a French knot at the end for each stamen.

completed flowers

Spangles

Requirements

fine silk thread: *YLI Silk Stitch #100 (col. 215)*

4 mm gold spangles

not actual size

Stitch gold spangles to the background with fine silk thread, making three stitches into each spangle (secure the thread behind each spangle before moving on to the next one). Position the spangles as desired.

Garland
OF SPRING
Flowers

Part Four

GARLAND OF SPRING FLOWERS

This pretty embroidered panel was inspired by the flowers of the spring garden and Shakespeare's tragic Ophelia.

Worked on a background of ivory satin in stumpwork and surface embroidery, this garland features the Wild Pansy, Viola tricolor, *with wired detached petals, beaded Forget-me-nots,* Myosotis arvensis, *raised Snowdrops,* Galanthus nivalis, *with wrapped stems, beaded calyx and detached petals, padded English Daisies,* Bellis perennis, *embroidered with detached chain stitches, and tiny bees.*

Opposite: not actual size (enlarged by 230%)

Skeleton outline

Diagram is actual size

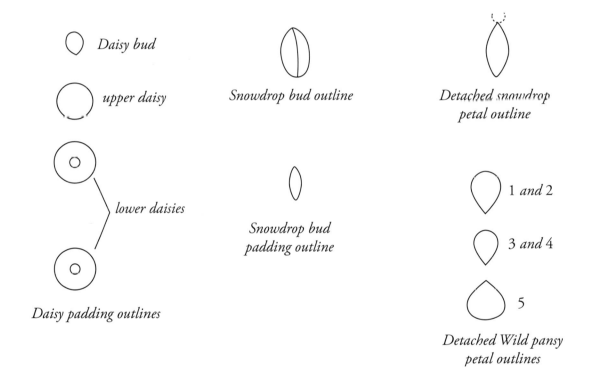

Daisy bud

upper daisy

lower daisies

Daisy padding outlines

Snowdrop bud outline

Snowdrop bud
padding outline

Detached snowdrop
petal outline

1 and 2

3 and 4

5

Detached Wild pansy
petal outlines

Diagrams are actual size

Ophelia's Flowers

In Hamlet, Shakespeare made extensive use of floral imagery when exploring the character of Ophelia, with flowers as symbols of memory, deep sorrow, faithfulness and innocence. The significance of these references would have been understood and appreciated by Elizabethan audiences.

Daisy illustration from MS Ashmole 1504,
Bodleian Library, Oxford (folios 7 & 7v)

There is a willow grows aslant a brook,

That shows his hoar leaves in the glassy stream:

Therewith fantastic garlands did she come

Of crow-flowers, nettles, daisies, and long purples,

That liberal shepherds give a grosser name,

But our cold maids do dead men's fingers call them:

There, on the pendent boughs her coronet weeds

Clambering to hang, an envious sliver broke;

When down the weedy trophies, and herself

Fell in the weeping brook. Her clothes spread wide;

And, mermaid-like, a while they bore her up:

Which time, she chanted snatches of old tunes;

As one incapable of her own distress,

Or like a creature native and indued

Unto that element: but long it could not be

Till her garment, heavy with their drink,

Pull'd the poor wretch from her melodious lay

To muddy death.

HAMLET (iv.7)

This is the complete list of requirements for this piece. For ease of use, the requirements for each individual element are repeated under its heading—for example, Snowdrops requirements.

- -

ivory satin: *20 cm (8 in) square*
quilter's muslin: *four 20 cm (8 in) squares*
tracing paper
white felt: *5 x 8 cm (2 x 3 in)*
paper-backed fusible web: *5 x 8 cm (2 x 3 in)*

---

25 cm (10 in) embroidery hoop or stretcher bars
10 and 15 cm (4 and 6 in) embroidery hoops
needles:
   crewel/embroidery sizes 5–10
   milliners/straw sizes 3–9
   sharp yarn darners sizes 14–18
embroidery equipment (see page 244)
nylon clear thread:
   Madeira Monofil 60 col. 1001

Stems & Leaves
dark green stranded thread:
   Soie d'Alger 2126 or DMC 987
medium green stranded thread:
   Soie d'Alger 2114 or DMC 988

English Daisy
dark pink stranded thread:
   Soie d'Alger 3022 or DMC 3688
medium pink stranded thread:
   Soie d'Alger 2931 or DMC 963
light pink stranded thread:
   Soie d'Alger 4147 or DMC 819
white stranded thread:
   Soie d'Alger Blanc or DMC White
medium yellow stranded thread:
   Soie d'Alger 543 or DMC 743
light green stranded thread:
   Soie d'Alger 231 or DMC 369
medium green stranded thread:
   Soie d'Alger 2114 or DMC 988

Forget-me-nots
dark green stranded thread:
   Soie d'Alger 2126 or DMC 987
medium green stranded thread:
   Soie d'Alger 2114 or DMC 988
medium blue stranded thread:
   Soie d'Alger 4913 or DMC 793
medium yellow stranded thread:
   Soie d'Alger 543 or DMC 743

Wild Pansy

medium mauve stranded thread:
Soie d'Alger 3323 (no match in DMC)
light mauve stranded thread:
Soie d'Alger 3322 (no match in DMC)
dark yellow stranded thread:
DMC 742 or Madeira Silk 114
medium yellow stranded thread:
DMC 743 or Soie d'Alger 543
light yellow stranded thread:
DMC 744 or Soie d'Alger 542
very pale yellow stranded thread:
DMC 745 or Soie d'Alger 2511
orange stranded thread:
DMC 741 or Soie d'Alger 546
dark purple fine silk thread:
YLI Silk Stitch 50 col. 24

Snowdrops

white stranded thread:
oie d'Alger Blanc (4096) or DMC White
light green stranded thread:
Soie d'Alger 231 or DMC 369
medium green stranded thread:
Soie d'Alger 2114 or DMC 988

Tiny Bees

old gold stranded thread:
DMC 783
black stranded thread:
DMC 310
silver/black metallic thread:
Kreinik Cord 105c

Mill Hill glass beads 128 (yellow)
Mill Hill frosted glass beads 60168 (mid-blue)
Mill Hill frosted glass beads 62034 (violet)
3 mm green pearl beads

33 gauge white covered wire (Wild Pansy detached petals): ten 9 cm (3½ in) lengths (if desired, colour two lengths yellow for the lower petals, Copic Y15 Cadmium Yellow)
28 gauge silver uncovered wire (Snowdrop detached petals): three 12 cm (5 in) lengths

1. Mount the satin background fabric and the muslin backing into the 15 cm (6 in) embroidery hoop. The fabrics need to be kept very taut.

2. Using a fine lead pencil, trace the skeleton outline of the design onto tracing paper. This will be the 'right side' of the tracing paper. Flip the tracing paper over and draw over the design outlines again on the back (do not make the lines too dark).

3. With the tracing paper 'right side' up, position the tracing over the satin, checking that the design is on the straight grain of the fabric. Temporarily secure the edges of the tracing paper to the satin with strips of masking tape. Using a stylus, draw over the design lines to transfer the skeleton outline of the design to the satin (it helps to have a board underneath the frame of fabric to provide a firm surface).

Note: Take care to use the minimum amount of lead when tracing. If your outlines are too dark, gently press the traced outlines with pieces of masking tape or Magic Tape to remove any excess graphite.

Daisy illustration from MS Ashmole 1504, Bodleian Library, Oxford (folios 7 & 7v)

Order of Work

1. Stems & Tendrils

2. Leaves

3. English Daisies

4. Forget-me-nots

5. Snowdrops

6. Wild Pansies

7. Tiny Bees

Requirements
dark green stranded thread:
Soie d'Alger 2126 or DMC 987

medium green stranded thread:
Soie d'Alger 2114 or DMC 988

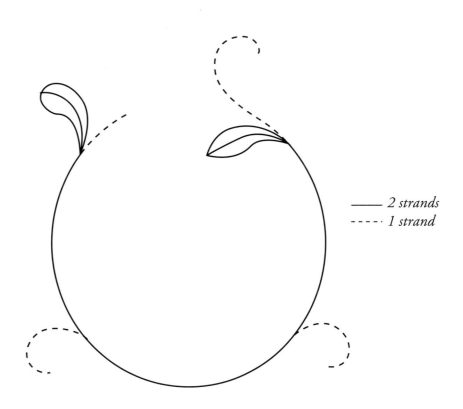

———— *2 strands*
- - - - *1 strand*

Reference only, diagram not actual size. See skeleton outline on page 202.

Stems & Tendrils

The main stems and tendrils are worked in chain stitch with dark green thread. The snowdrop stems are worked in medium green at a later stage.

1. Starting at the edge of the lower left small circle, work the left main stem in chain stitch with two strands of thread, reducing to one strand near the upper leaf to work the daisy bud stem.

2. Work the lower main stem, between the small circles, in chain stitch with two strands of thread, leaving a small gap at each of the lower circles to insert the detached wild pansy petals.

3. Starting at the edge of the lower right circle, work the right main stem in chain stitch with two strands of thread, reducing to one strand near the upper leaf to work the forget-me-not tendril.

4. Work the two lower forget-me-not tendrils in chain stitch with one strand of thread.

Note: The snowdrop stems will be worked at the same time as the flowers.

Leaves

1. Using one strand of medium green thread, work the central veins in chain stitch.

2. Starting with the outside edge, embroider each leaf with consecutive rows of stem stitch, using dark green thread for the three lower leaves, and medium green thread for the two upper leaves.

ENGLISH
Daisy

When daisies pied, and violets blue,
And lady-smocks all silver white,
And cuckoo-buds of yellow hue,
Do paint the meadows with delight.

Love's Labour's Lost (v.2)

The English Daisy, *Bellis perennis,* a perennial plant with rosettes of dark green, spoon-shaped leaves and small, button-like flowers in shades of white, pink and red, is also known as the Lawn Daisy, indicating its prevalence in meadows, lawns and grassy slopes almost all year round in England (*bellis* means 'pretty', and *perennis* 'everlasting', in Latin). Considered to be the flower of childhood and innocence, English Daisies were much loved by children for the making of daisy chains to be hung around the neck or worn as a garland in the hair.

The name 'daisy' is thought to have derived from the Anglo-Saxon *daes eage* (day's eye), because the flower head closes at night and opens in the morning. Geoffrey Chaucer claimed the daisy as his favourite flower, growing 'white and rede' in the flowery mead. He called it 'eye of the day'.

Daisies, among other wild flowers gathered from the riverside, are included in the 'fantastic garlands' featured in the tragic drowning of gentle, mad Ophelia.

The medicinal properties of the daisy were recorded as far back as the sixteenth century in Gerard's herbal. The flowers and leaves were used fresh in ointments and poultices for treating wounds, while a mild decoction of the flowers eased complaints of the respiratory tract:

The Daisies do mitigate all kindes of paines, but especially in the joints, and gout, if they be stamped with new butter unsalted, and applied upon the pained place ... The juice of the leaves and roots snift up into the nosthrils, purgeth the head mightily, and helpeth the megrim ... The decoction of the field Daisie made in water and drunke, is good against agues.

John Gerard, THE HERBALL (1597)

Designs for daisies by Jacques de Moyne de Morgues (1586) and Joan Drew (1929)

Daisy embroidery motif. (John Overton).

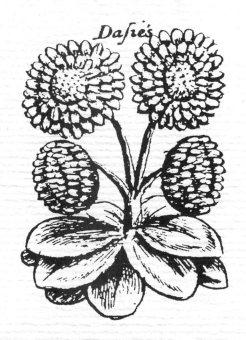

not actual size

Requirements

dark pink stranded thread:
Soie d'Alger 3022 or DMC 3688

medium pink stranded thread:
Soie d'Alger 2931 or DMC 963

light pink stranded thread:
Soie d'Alger 4147 or DMC 819

white stranded thread:
Soie d'Alger Blanc or DMC White

medium yellow stranded thread:
Soie d'Alger 543 or DMC 743

light green stranded thread:
Soie d'Alger 231 or DMC 369

medium green stranded thread:
Soie d'Alger 2114 or DMC 988

white felt: *5 x 8 cm (2 x 3 in)*

paper-backed fusible web:
5 x 8 cm (2 x 3 in)

Trace the three daisy padding outlines and one bud padding outline onto paper-backed fusible web, then fuse to the white felt. Cut out the padding shapes and remove the paper.

Daisy Flower

Each daisy is padded with one circle of felt, using the smaller circle for the upper daisy. Apply the felt with the fusible-web side up (to prevent the felt fibres from working their way through the stitches), lining up the centre circle of the felt padding with the small circle outline on the satin. The felt padding will be covered by four layers of detached chain stitches, all worked over the edge of the felt. Each layer consists of sixteen evenly spaced, detached chain stitches, worked with one strand of thread in a size 10 crewel needle. It is really important that the chain stitches are worked from the edge of the small inner circle, not from a central point, and that they are worked over the edge of the felt padding. Vary the length of the stitches a little, as the edges of English daisies are quite ragged in appearance.

1. The first layer of chain stitches is worked with dark pink thread. To hold the felt padding in position, work four chain stitches from the edge of the inner circle over the edge of the felt (as it is important that these stitches are evenly placed, work them at 'north', 'south', 'east' and 'west'). Then work three evenly spaced chain stitches in each segment—sixteen stitches in all. Use these first sixteen stitches as a guide to the even placement of the remaining layers of chain stitches.

2. Using medium pink thread, work sixteen chain stitches, slightly to the right of each of the dark pink stitches, starting the stitches at the edge of the inner circle and taking them over the edge of the felt.

3. Using light pink thread, work sixteen chain stitches, slightly to the left of each of the dark pink stitches, starting the stitches at the edge of the inner circle and taking them over the edge of the felt.

4. Work the final layer of sixteen chain stitches with white thread, making the stitches slightly shorter and quite 'loose', and working them over the medium pink stitches.

5. Using two strands of medium yellow thread, work the centre of the daisy with French knots (one wrap). First form a circle of knots, then build up the centre as desired. With one strand of light green thread, work a circle of French knots around the yellow centre.

completed flower

Daisy Bud

1. Using medium pink thread, apply the bud padding, fusible web side up, with small stab stitches. Work detached chain stitches over the top half of the bud, taking the stitches over the edge of the felt.

2. With dark pink thread, work chain stitches over the lower section of the bud, starting the stitches at the base and working them over the medium pink stitches, leaving the tips of medium pink visible at the top of the bud.

3. Using medium green thread, work approximately seven chain stitches over the petals to form the sepals, starting the stitches at the top of the stem and cupping them around the shape.

completed bud

Forget-me-nots

Myosotis (from Greek, meaning 'mouse's ear', referring to the furry leaf) is a genus of plants with small, flat, 5-lobed blue, pink or white flowers with yellow centres that are known as Forget-me-nots. This common name is derived from the French *ne m'oubliez pas* ('do not forget me') and was first used in English in the early sixteenth century. Similar names and variations are found in many languages. Henry IV took for his emblem a blue flower called *souveigne vous de moy* ('remember me') during his exile abroad in 1398, and retained it upon his return to England the following year.

Forget-me-not – symbol of love and faithfulness.

In medieval Europe, the little blue flowers of the Forget-me-not signified remembrance and were often worn by ladies as a sign of faithfulness and enduring love. There are several legends surrounding the name, the most romantic being from medieval times, where it is claimed that a knight and his lady were walking beside a river bank when, as he picked her a posy of flowers, the weight of his armour caused him to slip into the river. As he was drowning he threw the posy to his loved one and shouted 'Forget me not!' Another legend, recorded by Jenny de Gex in *Bible Flowers* (page 21) tells 'when the Creator thought he had finished giving the flowers their colours, he heard one whisper "Forget me not!" There was nothing left but a very small amount of blue, but the forget-me-not was delighted to wear such a light blue shade'.

Forget-me-nots were frequently used by illuminators of medieval manuscripts to provide a splash of brilliant blue in their painted borders.

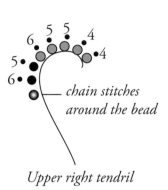

Upper right tendril

chain stitches around the bead

not actual sizes

Requirements

dark green stranded thread:
Soie d'Alger 2126 or DMC 987

medium green stranded thread:
Soie d'Alger 2114 or DMC 988

medium blue stranded thread:
Soie d'Alger 4913 or DMC 793

medium yellow stranded thread:
Soie d'Alger 543 or DMC 743

nylon clear thread:
Madeira Monofil 60 col. 1001

Mill Hill glass beads 128 *(yellow)*

Mill Hill frosted glass beads 60168 *(mid-blue)*

Mill Hill frosted glass beads 62034 *(violet)*

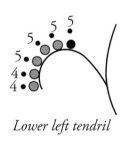

Lower left tendril

FORGET-ME-NOT BUDS GUIDE

- • *French knots showing number of strands*
- 🔘 *medium green*
- ● *blue*
- ⦿ *blue bead*

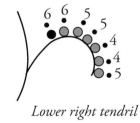

Lower right tendril

The forget-me-not tendrils are worked in chain stitch with one strand of dark green thread.

Forget-me-not Buds

The buds on the tendrils are worked with French knots, using medium green or medium blue thread, or a bead. Work the French knots with one wrap, using six, five, four or three strands of thread as shown in the diagrams. The bead is applied with blue thread. The tiny leaves around the larger buds are worked in fly stitch or chain stitch with two strands of medium green thread.

Note: I worked the French knots requiring six strands of thread first, then removed one thread at a time to work the remaining knots (park the 'removed' threads at the back and secure at the end). A different combination of threads has been used for each tendril.

Forget-me-not Flowers

1. Using nylon thread, stitch a yellow bead in the centre of the flower (over the dots marked on the satin), working three or four stitches into the bead (the hole in the bead facing up, like a doughnut).

2. With one strand of medium blue thread, stitch five blue beads around the yellow centre bead, stitching from the outside towards the centre (the holes of the beads face the centre). Work a second stitch through each blue bead. Work some flowers with violet beads, and some with mid-blue.

3. Using one strand of medium yellow thread, work a French knot (two wraps) in the centre of each yellow bead.

Wild Pansies

The much loved Wild Pansy, *Viola tricolor*, which grew wild in gardens as well as in the fields, is also known as Heartsease, Love-in-Idleness and Johnny-jump-up. The French called them *pensées*, meaning 'thoughts' (the origin of pansy). While they can vary a great deal in size and colour, Wild Pansies are usually purple, yellow or white, often with a combination of all three colours in each flower (hence the Latin species name). The upper petals are generally most eyecatching—often a shade of purple, while the lowest and broadest petal is usually a more or less deep tint of yellow. The flower protects itself from rain and dew by drooping its head both at night and in wet weather, thus the back of the flower and not its face receives the moisture.

Shakespeare liked to use flowers and plants as images to illustrate his ideas. In *Hamlet*, Ophelia passes out flowers to the court—an indirect (and safe) way of indicating her deep sorrow and grief at the murder of her father:

> There's rosemary, that's for remembrance;
>   pray, love, remember:
>   and there is pansies, that's for thoughts.
>   HAMLET (iv.5)

Ophelia refers here to the Wild Pansy, the symbol for thought and faithfulness.

WILD PANSIES : METHOD

Requirements

medium mauve stranded thread:
Soie d'Alger 3323 (no match in DMC)

light mauve stranded thread:
Soie d'Alger 3322 (no match in DMC)

dark yellow stranded thread:
DMC 742 or Madeira Silk 114

medium yellow stranded thread:
DMC 743 or Soie d'Alger 543

light yellow stranded thread:
DMC 744 or Soie d'Alger 542

very pale yellow stranded thread:
DMC 745 or Soie d'Alger 2511

orange stranded thread:
DMC 741 or Soie d'Alger 546

dark purple fine silk thread:
YLI Silk Stitch 50 col. 24

quilter's muslin:
two 20 cm (8 in) squares

33 gauge white covered wire (detached petals):
*ten 9 cm (3½ in) lengths (if desired, colour two
lengths yellow for the lower petals, Copic Y15
Cadmium Yellow)*

not actual size

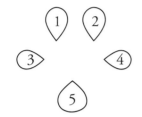

Mount the muslin into a small hoop and trace five detached petals for the left wild pansy and five detached petals for the right wild pansy. Number them from 1 to 5 as indicated. The petals are embroidered with one strand of thread in a size 10 crewel needle.

Left Wild Pansy

PETALS 1 AND 2

1. Using one strand of medium mauve thread, and starting at the base of the petal, couch a length of wire around the petal outline, crossing the wire tails at the base (trim the 'underneath' wire to 3 mm retaining one long wire tail with which to attach the petal). Buttonhole stitch the wire to the muslin.

2. Using medium mauve thread, work a row of long and short buttonhole stitch inside the wire at the top edge of the petal (this row of stitching will come about halfway down the petal). Embroider the remainder of the petal in long and short stitch, blending light mauve thread in to the medium mauve.

PETALS 3 & 4

1. Using one strand of light mauve thread, couch a length of wire around the petal outline, crossing the wire tails at the base (trim the 'underneath' wire to 3 mm, retaining one long wire tail). Buttonhole-stitch the wire to the muslin.

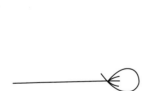

2. Using light mauve thread, work a row of long and short buttonhole stitch inside the wire at the top edge of the petal. Embroider the remainder of the petal in long and short stitch, blending light yellow into the light mauve.

3. With one strand of dark purple silk thread in a size 12 sharps needle, work three straight stitches at the base of the petal to form rays.

PETAL 5

1. Using medium yellow thread, couch a length of wire (coloured yellow if desired) around the petal outline, leaving two wire tails, of equal length, that touch but do not cross. Buttonhole-stitch the wire to the muslin.

2. Using medium yellow thread, work a row of long and short buttonhole stitch inside the wire at the top edge of the petal. Embroider the remainder of the petal in long and short stitch, blending dark yellow into the medium yellow.

3. With one strand of dark purple silk thread in a size 12 sharps needle, work five straight stitches (of varying lengths) at the base of the petal to form rays, leaving a small space at the inner corner of the petal.

completed flower

Right Wild Pansy

PETALS 1 AND 2

Work as for the left wild pansy.

PETALS 3 AND 4

1. Using very pale yellow thread, couch a length of wire around the petal outline, crossing the wire tails at the base (trim the 'underneath' wire to 3 mm retaining one wire tail). Buttonhole-stitch the wire to the muslin.

2. Using light yellow thread, work a row of long and short buttonhole stitch inside the wire at the top edge of the petal. Embroider the remainder of the petal in long and short stitch, blending medium yellow thread into the light yellow.

3. With one strand of dark purple silk thread in a size 12 sharps needle, work three straight stitches at the base of the petal to form rays.

PETAL 5

1. Using medium yellow thread, couch a length of wire (coloured yellow if desired) around the petal outline, leaving two wire tails, of equal length, that touch but do not cross. Buttonhole-stitch the wire to the muslin.

2. Using dark yellow thread, work a row of long and short buttonhole stitch inside the wire at the top edge of the petal. Embroider the remainder of the petal in long and short stitch, blending orange into the dark yellow.

3. With one strand of dark purple silk thread in a size 12 sharps needle, work five straight stitches (of varying lengths) at the base of the petal to form rays, leaving a small space at the inner corner of the petal.

To Complete the Wild Pansy

1. Carefully cut out the petals close to the buttonholed edge. For petals 1–4, trim the short wire tails close to the stitching, being careful not to cut the remaining wire tail.

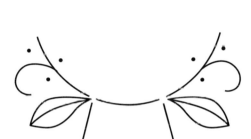

2. Using a large yarn darner, insert the five petals of the left pansy through the small gap in the left side of the lower main stem. Apply the petals in the order as numbered (petal 5 is applied last), securing the wire tails to the muslin behind each petal with small stitches using white thread (it is easier to secure each petal before proceeding to the next). Separate the two wire tails for petal 5 (like an upside-down V) and secure individually to stop the petal moving when finally shaped. Apply the petals for the right pansy through the small gap on the right of the lower main stem. Do not trim the wires until the centre is worked.

*left wire
insertion point*   *right wire
insertion point*

3. With six strands of orange thread in a chenille needle, work the centre of each pansy with a French knot (one loose wrap), worked into the 'hole' between the petals. Carefully shape the petals with tweezers then trim the wire tails.

*completed
flower*

Snowdrops

The Snowdrop, *Galanthus nivalis,* is a perennial bulb with narrow, grey-green leaves, and a solitary, nodding, white, bell-shaped flower with three outer petals and three smaller inner ones, often with a green marking at the tip. One of the most popular of all cultivated bulbous plants, the flowering of the common Snowdrop is traditionally seen to herald the end of winter:

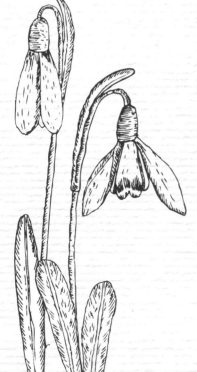

Thou first-born of the year's delight, pride of the dewy glade,
In vernal green and virgin white thy vestal robes arrayed ....
They twinkle to the wintry moon, and cheer the ungenial day,
And tell us, all will glisten soon as green and bright as they.
   John Keble, 1827

The name *Galanthus* ('milk-white flowers' in Latin) was given to the genus by Carl Linnaeus in 1735, and the description *nivalis* ('of the snow') was a reference to both the colour of the flower and its early flowering. The common name, Snowdrop, first appeared in the 1633 edition of Gerard's herbal—in the first edition he had described it as the 'Timely flowring Bulbus Violet':

The Bulbous Violet riseth out of the ground, with two small leaves flat and crested, of an overworne greene colour, betweene the which riseth up a small and tender stalke of two hands high; at the top whereof commeth forth of a skinny hood a small white floure of the bignesse of a Violet, compact of six leaves, three bigger, and three lesser, tipped at the points with light greene; the smaller are fashioned into the vulgar forme of an heart, and prettily edged about with green; the other three leaves are longer, and sharpe pointed. The whole floure hangeth down his head, by reason of the weake foot-stalke whereon it groweth. They are maintained and cherished in gardens for the beautie and rarenesse of the floures, and sweetnesse of their smell.

John Gerard, *THE HERBALL* (1633 edition)

Originally known as Candlemas Bells, Snowdrops acquired a religious significance because their February flowering (in the northern hemisphere) coincided with Candlemas, the feast of the purification of the Virgin, which included the scattering of white flowers before her image in candlelight. Drifts of naturalised snowdrops mark the sites of long-forgotten monasteries and churchyards to this day, reinforcing the idea of monks and pilgrims returning with snowdrop bulbs from journeys to Rome and beyond.

not actual size

Requirements

white stranded thread:
Soie d'Alger Blanc (4096) or DMC White

light green stranded thread:
Soie d'Alger 231 or DMC 369

medium green stranded thread:
Soie d'Alger 2114 or DMC 988

nylon clear thread:
Madeira Monofil 60 col. 1001

quilter's muslin:
two 20 cm squares

white felt:
5 x 8 cm (2 x 3 in)

paper-backed fusible web:
5 x 8 cm (2 x 3 in)

3 mm green pearl beads

28 gauge silver uncovered wire:
three 12 cm (5 in) lengths

Snowdrop Flower

SNOWDROP BACKGROUND PETAL

1. With one strand of medium green thread, work the snowdrop stem with small chain stitches, stopping one stitch before the wire insertion point • (at the end of the stem): keep the thread on the surface (parked to the side) to use later.

2. Outline the snowdrop background petal in back stitch with one strand of white thread. Work a row of close, long and short buttonhole stitch around the lower edge of the petal, enclosing the back stitch outline. Embroider the remainder of the petal in long and short stitch. This petal will be underneath the two detached petals.

SNOWDROP DETACHED PETALS

Work two detached petals for each snowdrop. To avoid soiling the white edges of the petals with a traced pencil outline, the wires are bent into a petal shape first, before applying to the muslin. Use tweezers, and the detached petal outline as a template, to bend the wires into the required petal shapes.

1. Mount muslin into a small hoop. Shape a 12 cm (5 in) length of uncovered wire around the detached petal outline, leaving two tails of wire at the base that touch but do not cross. Make the tails of wire equal in length and do not trim. They will be wrapped later to form the arched pedicel (stem) at the top of the flower. (I used uncovered wire for these petals as it was the only wire fine enough to thread through the green pearls.)

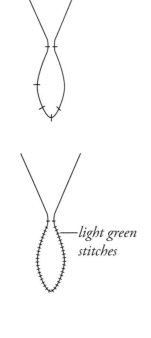

—*light green stitches*

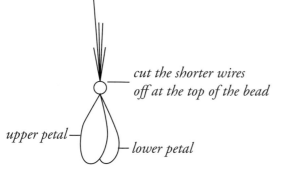

shorten one end

green thread

cut the shorter wires
off at the top of the bead

upper petal —

— *lower petal*

2. Using one strand of white thread and starting at the base of the petal (working separate stitches over each wire at the base), couch then overcast the shaped wire to the muslin. Using a new length of white thread, embroider the petal in long and short stitch, adding a blush of light green at the base of the petal. Work four petals (two for each flower).

To Complete the Snowdrop Flower

Each snowdrop has two detached petals. When applied, one will overlap the other—they will be referred to as the upper and lower petal. The wire tails of the detached bud petals are inserted through a green pearl then wrapped with medium green thread to form the pedicel. This is shaped into a smooth curve then inserted at the top of the snowdrop stem.

1. Cut out the two detached flower petals. As the petals will overlap each other to form the flower, select one to be the upper petal. Cut a 40 cm (16 in) length of medium green thread and attach to the back of the lower petal, near the wire tails (this thread will be used for wrapping the wires). Place the upper petal over the lower petal, bring the needle and green thread out at the very top of both petals (between the wires), and then through a green bead.

2. Now insert the four wire tails through the green bead. Arrange the petals so that the upper petal is above the lower, and shape slightly. Cut off two wire tails close to the top of the bead—one wire from each petal.

Hint: cut one wire from each petal shorter first to identify them.

3. Bend the remaining lower petal wire at right angles to the bead (this holds the bead in place). Wrap the remaining upper petal wire with the green thread for at least 1 cm (½ in) to form the wrapped detached pedicel (stem); it is advisable to wrap a little longer than required.

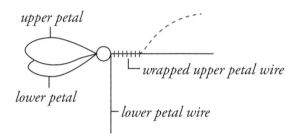

upper petal

lower petal

wrapped upper petal wire

lower petal wire

4. Apply the two detached petals to the main fabric (over the embroidered background petal) as follows:

(i) Using a yarn darner, insert the lower petal wire through a point 'one green bead width' above the background petal, and hold at the back with masking tape until the upper petal wire is inserted.

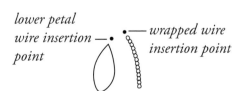

lower petal wire insertion point

wrapped wire insertion point

(ii) Insert the wrapped upper petal wire at the top of the chain stitched stem • , shaping into a curve with tweezers. Hold at the back with masking tape.

(iii) Secure the lower petal wire to the back of the embroidered background petal with small stitches using white thread.

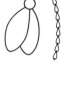

(iv) Using the parked medium green thread (one strand), work a chain stitch around the wire entry point, then, with two strands of green thread, make a long chain stitch from the wire entry point to form the spathe around the stem. Secure. (The spathe is the pair of narrow green bracts which curve behind the pedicel of the snowdrop.)

(v) Secure the wrapped wire tail to the back of the stem and trim. Shape the petals and wrapped pedicel with tweezers. If required, make invisible stitches into the top and side edges of the petals to hold them in place, using nylon thread.

completed flowers

Snowdrop Bud

The embroidered snowdrop bud is applied to the satin over felt padding.

1. With one strand of medium green thread, work the snowdrop bud stem with small chain stitches, stopping one stitch before the wire insertion point • (at the end of the stem); keep the thread on the surface (parked to the side) to use later.

2. To pad the bud, cut a piece of white felt slightly smaller than the bud outline, and stab stitch to the background, inside the traced outline, using white thread.

3. Trace the snowdrop bud shape onto muslin. Using one strand of white thread, couch then overcast a length of uncovered wire along the central line of bud, leaving a wire tail at each end. Outline the bud in split back stitch, then embroider in long and short stitch, adding a blush of pale green at the stem end of the bud (upper wire).

4. With one strand of white thread, work a row of running stitch around the embroidered shape, about 1.5 mm away from the edge. Start near the upper wire tails and take the running stitches under the lower tail of wire, leaving two tails of thread on the front.

5. Cut out the shape, about 1.5 mm away from the running stitches, avoiding the tails of thread and wire.

light green stitches

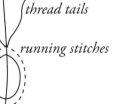

thread tails

running stitches

To Complete the Bud

1. Gently pull the tails of gathering thread to draw up the edges and finger-press the seam allowance under the bud.

2. To apply the bud, insert the lower wire at the lower edge of the padded outline and tape to the back (secure later). With one strand of white thread, stab stitch the bud in place, using the outline as a guide and leaving the upper wire free. Work some straight stitches around the bud to cover the stab stitches if required.

3. Thread one strand of medium green thread into a fine needle and bring out at the top of the bud, near the upper wire. Wrap the upper wire for at least 1 cm (½ in) and secure. Thread a green bead over the wrapped wire.

4. Insert the wrapped bud wire at the top of the chain-stitched stem • , shaping into a curve with tweezers. Hold at the back with masking tape. Complete as for the snowdrop flowers. The green bead may be secured with an invisible stitch with nylon thread, if required.

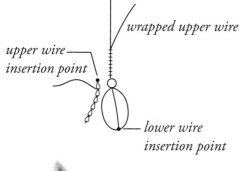

upper wire—
insertion point

wrapped upper wire

lower wire
insertion point

*completed
bud*

Tiny Bees

Requirements

old gold stranded thread: *DMC 783*

black stranded thread: *DMC 310*

silver/black metallic thread: *Kreinik Cord 105c*

not actual size

1. Using one strand of black thread, work seven satin stitches 3 mm (1/8 in) in length to pad the abdomen of the bee, working the stitches into the same two holes at each end of the marked line.

2. Using one strand of black thread and one strand of old gold thread, work satin stitches over the padded body to form the striped abdomen, working two satin stitches for each stripe. First work a black stripe in the centre of the abdomen, then a gold stripe on either side, finishing with a black stripe at each end.

3. With one strand of black thread, work a French knot (two wraps) at one end of the abdomen for the head.

4. Using one strand of silver/black thread, work two detached chain stitches for the wings.

PART FIVE

TECHNIQUES
Equipment
& Stitch Glossary

This section contains general information about the techniques
and equipment that are referred to throughout the book.

The stitch glossary includes the stitches used.

The bibliography contains a list of specialised reference books
which can provide more detailed information if required.

MOUNTING FABRICS

Mounting Fabric into an Embroidery Hoop

Good quality embroidery hoops—10 cm, 12 cm, 15 cm, 20 cm and 25 cm (4 in, 5 in, 6 in, 8 in and 10 in) diameter—are essential when working small to medium size designs in stumpwork embroidery. Bind the inner ring of wooden hoops with cotton tape to prevent slipping. A small screwdriver is useful to tighten the embroidery hoop. Plastic hoops with a lip on the inner ring are also suitable (because of the lip the inner ring does not need to be bound).

1. Place the main (background) fabric on top of the backing fabric then place both fabrics over the inner ring of the hoop. If using a plastic hoop, make sure that the lip-edge of the hoop is uppermost.

2. Loosen the outer ring of the hoop so that it just fits over the inner ring and the fabrics, positioning the tension screw at the top of the hoop (12 o'clock). Ease the outer ring down over the inner ring and fabrics.

3. To tension the fabrics in the hoop, pull the fabrics evenly and tighten the screw, alternately, until both layers of fabric are as tight as a drum in the hoop. If using the plastic hoop, the fabric-covered lip-edge of the inner ring should sit just above the top edge of the outer ring. In stumpwork, the fabrics are not removed from the hoop until the embroidery is finished.

Mounting fabric into square or rectangular frames

A square or rectangular frame is required for larger designs in stumpwork embroidery. An artist's stretcher bar frame, a slate frame or a tapestry frame may be used (I use a slate frame).

❋ **TO ATTACH THE BACKGROUND AND BACKING FABRIC TO A STRETCHER BAR FRAME**

1. Assemble the stretcher bars.

2. Staple or pin (drawing pin/push pin) the background fabric and the calico *together* to the back of one long side of the frame.

3. Stretch and staple or pin the calico *then* the background fabric to the back of the other long side of the frame (fabrics stretched and secured separately).

4. Staple or pin the background fabric and the calico *together* to the back of one short side of the frame.

5. Stretch and staple or pin the calico *then* the background fabric to the back of the remaining short side of the frame.

❋ **TO ATTACH THE BACKGROUND AND BACKING FABRICS TO A SLATE FRAME OR TAPESTRY FRAME**

1. Select a frame with internal measurements at least 10–15 cm (4–6 in) larger than the required background fabric.

2. To prepare the backing fabric, cut a piece of firm calico or muslin 2 cm (1 in) narrower than the internal width of the frame (the roll bar and webbing) and about 10 cm (4 in) longer than the internal length of the frame. Make sure the fabric is cut on the straight grain.

3. Finish all edges of the calico by first turning under 5 mm (¼ in) then folding over a 1 cm (½ in) hem. Stitch the hem by hand or machine (a length of fine string may be inserted in the hem of the side edges for extra strength— this is not necessary for smaller embroideries).

4. Mark the centre points of the webbing and calico. With right sides facing and centre points aligned, overcast the top edge of the calico to the webbing edge of one roll bar. Use a double strand of sewing thread and work from the centre point to each end, with the stitches about 5 mm (¼ in) apart. Repeat for the lower roll bar.

5. Assemble the slate frame (or tapestry frame), adjusting the roll bars so that the calico is smooth and taut—not drum tight.

6. Lace the side edges of the calico to the side edges of the frame, using a strong thread (e.g. Cotton Pearl 5 or fine string) still connected to the spool to avoid joins. Make the stitches about 2–3 cm (1 in) apart, leaving a long tail of thread at each end. Adjust the lacing to tighten the calico slightly—not drum tight yet. Secure the ends of the lacing thread temporarily.

7. Centre the background fabric (e.g. silk) over the calico, taking care to align the grains of both fabrics (a little masking tape can be used to hold the silk in place until secured with stitches). With one strand of sewing thread, sew the background fabric to the calico with herringbone stitch, working one edge of the stitch into the background fabric and the other edge into the calico. Start in the centre of the top edge and work to each corner. Repeat for the lower edge, then the sides. (Do not make the stitches too small or too even!)

8. Tighten the upper and lower bars of the frame, then adjust and secure the lacing on each side so that both layers of fabric are drum tight.

Cake decorator's wire is used to form the detached, wired and embroidered shapes characteristic of stumpwork. I find the following gauges the most useful.

❋ 33-GAUGE COVERED WIRE

A fine wire with a tightly wrapped, thin white paper covering which can be coloured if desired. This wire is used for small detached shapes, such as butterfly wings and flower petals.

❋ 28-GAUGE UNCOVERED WIRE

Uncovered wire (silver in colour) is used when a finer edge is required. Use it for small and detailed detached shapes, such as lacewing and moth wings.

To Stitch Wire to Fabric

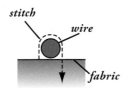

stitch
wire
fabric

cross section of fabric,
wire & stitch

When stitching wire to fabric, either with overcast stitch or buttonhole stitch, make sure that the needle enters the fabric *at right angles, very close to the wire* (not angled under the wire). The stitches need to be worked very close together, with an up-and-down stabbing motion, using a firm and even tension.

If you need to renew a thread while stitching wire to fabric, secure the thread tails inside the wired shape (do not use a knot at the edge as it may be cut when cutting out the shape). If you need to renew a thread while stitching wire for a wing, you cannot secure the thread inside the wired shape. Instead, hold the tail of the old thread and the tail of the new thread under the length of wire about to be stitched. Catch both tails of thread in with the new overcast stitches.

Using very sharp scissors with fine points, cut out the wired shape as close to the stitching as possible (stroke the cut edge with your fingernail to reveal any stray threads). If you happen to cut a stitch, use the point of a pin to apply a minute amount of PVA glue to the cut thread. This will dry matt and clear.

To Colour Wire

White paper-covered wire may be coloured with a waterproof ink if desired. *This is optional.* When I colour wires I use Copic markers, which are available from art supply stores. These markers are fast-drying and refillable and come in a huge range of colours.

To Attach Wired Shapes to a Background Fabric

Detached wire shapes are applied to a background fabric by inserting the wire tails through a 'tunnel' formed by the eye of a large (size 14) sharp yarn darner needle.

1. Pierce the background fabric at the required point with the yarn darner and push it through until the *eye* of the needle is half-way through the fabric (this forms a 'tunnel' through to the back of the fabric).

2. Insert the wire tails into the 'tunnel' formed by the eye of the darner, through to the *back of the fabric.* Thread tails can also be taken through at the same time.

3. Gently pull the darner all the way through, leaving the wire tails in the hole.

4. Stitch the wire tails to the backing fabric with small stitches, preferably behind an embroidered area (make sure the securing stitches will be hidden behind embroidery or underneath a detached shape).

5. Use tweezers to shape the detached petal or wing as required then trim the wire tails. I do not cut any wire tails until the subject is finished (just in case you need to unpick and re-do). Do not let any wire tails protrude into an unembroidered area as they may show when the piece is framed.

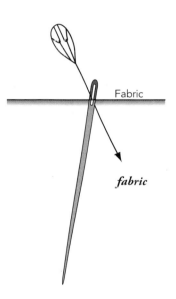

Fabric

fabric

cross section of fabric, yarn darner & wired shape

Paper-backed fusible web (also known as Vliesofix, Bondaweb and other brand names) is used to fuse or bond one material to another by applying heat with an iron. I also use paper-backed fusible web to obtain a precise design outline on felt—it is very difficult to trace a small shape on to felt and to cut it out accurately.

To Fuse a Design Outline to Felt

1. Trace the outline on to the paper side of the fusible web then fuse to the felt (fusible web/glue side down) with a medium-hot dry iron.

2. Cut out the shape along the outlines. Remove the paper before stitching the felt shape to the background fabric (e.g. flower padding).

Glossary

OF PRODUCT NAMES

*This list gives equivalent names for products used
throughout this book which may not be available
under the same name in every country.*

biro	=	ballpoint pen
calico	=	muslin
clutch pencil	=	mechanical pencil
GLAD Bake	=	baking parchment
quilter's muslin	=	finely woven calico
		or cotton homespun
paper-backed fusible web	=	Vliesofix, Bondaweb

The embroiderer's workbox should contain the following equipment:

- Good quality embroidery hoops:
  10 cm, 12 cm, 15 cm, 20 cm and 25 cm (4 in, 5 in, 6 in, 8 in and 10 in)
  diameter. Bind the inner ring of wooden hoops with cotton tape to prevent
  slipping. A small screwdriver is useful to tighten the embroidery hoops.
  Plastic hoops with a lip on the inner ring are also suitable.

- Slate frames in various sizes for larger embroideries

- Wooden tracing boards of various sizes: to place under hoops of fabric
  when tracing

- Needles:
  crewel/embroidery sizes 3–10, milliners/straw sizes 1–9, tapestry sizes
  26–28, sharps sizes 10–12, sharp yarn darners sizes 14–18

- Thimble

- Beeswax

- Fine glass-headed pins

- Embroidery scissors (small, with fine sharp points),
  goldwork scissors (small and strong with sharp points)
  and paper scissors

- Small wire-cutters or old scissors for cutting wire

- Mellor or old metal nailfile
  (for easing threads or leather into place)

- Assortment of tweezers
  (from surgical suppliers)

- Eyebrow comb
  (for Turkey knots)

- Tracing paper
  (I use GLAD Bake/baking parchment)

- Fine *(0.5 mm)* HB lead pencil *(mechanical)*

- Clover tracer pen, stylus or used ballpoint pen
  (for tracing)

- Masking tape
  (for tracing and to hold threads and wire tails to the back of the fabric)

- Post-it notes or 'removable' self-adhesive labels
  (for templates)

- Rulers—15 and 30 cm
  (6 and 12 in)

STITCH GLOSSARY

This glossary contains most of the stitches used in this book, in alphabetical order.

For ease of explanation, some of the stitches have been illustrated with the needle entering and leaving the fabric in the same movement. When working in a hoop this is difficult (or should be if your fabric is tight enough), so the stitches have to be worked with a stabbing motion, in several stages.

Back Stitch

This is a useful stitch for outlining a shape. Bring the needle out at 1, insert at 2 (sharing the hole made by the preceding stitch) and out again at 3. Keep the stitches small and even.

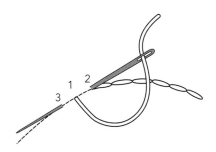

Back Stitch, Split

See Split Back Stitch

Buttonhole Stitch

These stitches can be worked close together or slightly apart. Working from left to right, bring the needle out on the line to be worked at 1 and insert at 2, holding the loop of thread with the left thumb. Bring the needle up on the line to be worked at 3 (directly below 2), over the thread loop and pull through to form a looped edge. If the stitch is shortened and worked close together over wire, it forms a secure edge for cut shapes, for example, detached petals.

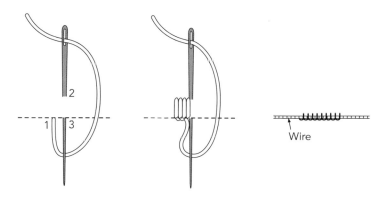

Buttonhole Stitch, Long and Short

In long and short buttonhole stitch, each alternate stitch is shorter. Bring the needle out at 1, insert at 2 and up again at 3 (like an open detached chain stitch). When embroidering a shape like a petal, angle the stitches towards the centre of the flower.

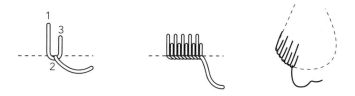

Buttonhole Stitch, Detached

Buttonhole stitch can be worked as a detached filling, attached only to the background material at the edges of the shape. First work a row of back stitches around the shape to be filled. Change to a fine tapestry needle. Bring the needle out at 1, work buttonhole stitches in to the top row of back stitches then insert the needle at 2. Come up again at 3 and work a buttonhole stitch into each loop of the preceding row. Insert the needle at 4. Quite different effects can be achieved when these stitches are worked close together or spaced apart.

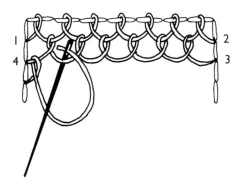

Buttonhole Stitch, Corded Detached

Detached buttonhole stitch can be worked over a laid thread. Outline the shape
to be filled with back stitches (or couch a wire frame to a buttonhole pad).
Using a tapestry needle, come up at 1 and work the first row of buttonhole
stitches into the top row of back stitches (or over the wire frame). Slip the
needle under the back stitch at 2 (or around the wire). Take the needle straight
back to the left side and slip under the back stitch at 3. Work another row of
buttonhole stitches, this time taking the needle into the previous loops *and*
under the straight thread at the same time. Slip the needle under the back
stitch at 4 and continue as above. A contrasting thread (or gold thread), worked
in another needle, can replace the straight thread, with interesting results.

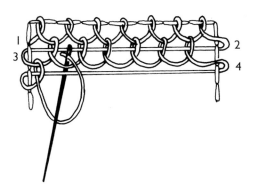

Chain Stitch

Bring the needle out at 1 and insert it again through the same hole, holding the loop of thread with the left thumb. Bring the needle up a short distance away at 2, through the loop, and pull the thread through. Insert the needle into the same hole at 2 (inside the loop) and make a second loop, hold, and come up at 3. Repeat to work a row of chain stitch, securing the final loop with a small straight stitch.

Chain Stitch, Broad
(also known as Reverse Chain Stitch)

Bring the needle through at the beginning of the line to be worked and make a short running stitch from 1 to 2 (the running stitch is only required to start the stitch). Bring the needle out at 3 (the desired length of the chain stitch), slide the needle back under the running stitch then into the fabric again at 4, leaving a small gap between 3 and 4 (or into the same hole if a narrower line is required). Bring the needle out at 5 (the length of the stitch), slide the needle under the loops of the first chain stitch then into the fabric again at 6, and so on. Note: when passing under the chain loops, the needle does not enter the fabric. It helps to use the eye of the needle for this stage of the stitch.

Chain Stitch, Detached (Lazy Daisy Stitch)

Detached chain stitch, also known as lazy daisy stitch, is worked in the same way as chain stitch except that each loop is secured individually with a small straight stitch. The securing stitch can be made longer if desired, for example, in a butterfly's antennae. Several detached chain stitches can be worked inside each other to pad a small shape.

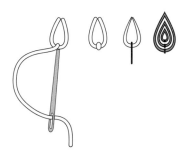

Chain Stitch, Interlaced

This stitch, when interlaced with a gold or contrasting thread, forms a very pretty braid. Work a row of chain stitch, or broad chain stitch, as a foundation, with two or three strands of thread. Interlace the right side of this chain stitch with gold or contrasting thread in a tapestry needle, as follows:

(a) Come out at 1, slide the needle under the right side of the second chain at 2.

(b) Slide the needle under the right side of the first chain *and* the gold thread at 3.

(c) Slide the needle under the right side of the next chain at 4.

(d) Slide the needle under both the right side of the chain and the gold thread at 5.

(e) Repeat the last two steps to the end of the row. Take the thread to the back of the work at the end of the last chain and secure.

To interlace the other side of the row of chain stitch, bring the needle out at 1 and work as above, reversing the direction of the needle.

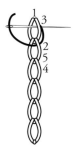

Couching

Couching is used to attach a thread, or bundle of threads, to a background fabric by means of small, vertical stitches worked at regular intervals. The laid thread is often thicker or more fragile than the one used for stitching. Couching stitches are also used for attaching wire to the base fabric before embroidering detached shapes.

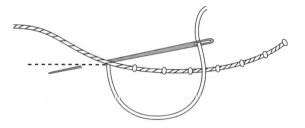

Feather Stitch

This stitch is made up of a series of loops, stitched alternately to the right and to the left, each one holding the previous loop in place. Come up on the line to be followed at 1. Insert the needle to the right at 2 and come up on the line again at 3, holding the thread under the needle with the left thumb. Repeat on the left side of the line, reversing the needle direction.

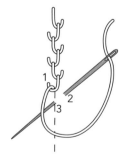

Feather Stitch, Single

Work the feather stitch loops in one direction only, either to the right or to the left. This variation is useful for working the veins in dragonfly wings.

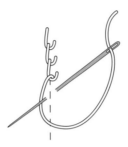

Fishbone Stitch

This stitch is useful for filling small leaf shapes. Bring the thread out at the tip of the leaf at 1, and make a small straight stitch along the centre line (vein). Bring the needle out at 2, make a slanted stitch and go down on the right of the centre line. Bring the needle out at 3, make a slanted stitch and go down on the left of the centre line, overlapping the base of the previous stitch. Continue working slanted stitches alternately from left and right, close together, until the shape is filled.

  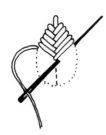

Fly Stitch

Fly stitch is actually an open detached chain stitch. Bring the needle out at 1 and insert at 2, holding the working thread with the left thumb. Bring up again at 3 and pull through over the loop. Secure the loop with either a short anchoring stitch, as for antennae, or a longer anchoring stitch as, for example, the veins in butterfly wings.

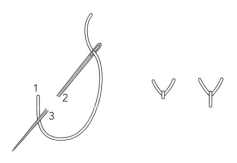

French Knot

Using a milliners/straw needle, bring the thread through at the desired place, wrap the thread once around the point of the needle and re-insert the needle. Tighten the thread and *hold taut* while pulling the needle through. To increase the size of the knot use more strands of thread, although more wraps can be made if desired.

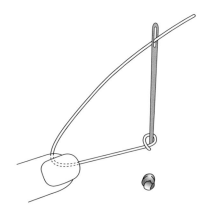

Long and Short Stitch

This stitch can be used to fill areas too large or irregular for satin stitch, or where shading is required. The first row, worked around the outline, consists of alternating long and short satin stitches (or long and short buttonhole stitch may be used). In the subsequent rows, the stitches are all of similar length, and fit into the spaces left by the preceding row. For a more realistic result when working petals, direct the stitches towards the centre of the flower. The surface will look smoother if the needle either pierces the stitches of the preceding row or enters at an angle between the stitches.

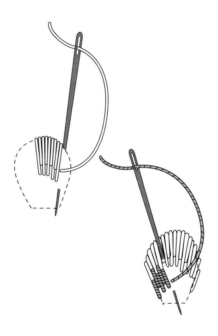

Long and Short Buttonhole Stitch
See Buttonhole Stitch, Long and Short

Needleweaving

Needleweaving is a form of embroidery where thread in a tapestry needle is woven in and out over two or more threads attached to the background fabric. Work needleweaving over a loop to form sepals, for example, bramble berries. Use a length of scrap thread to keep the loop taut while weaving.

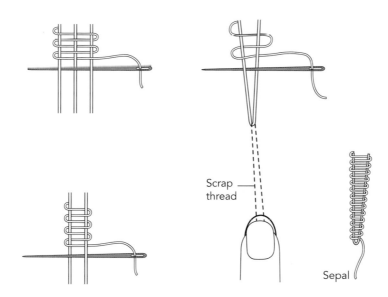

Scrap thread

Sepal

Outline Stitch

Worked from left to right, this stitch is perfect for working both simple and complicated outlines. Worked in the same way as stem stitch, the only difference is that the working thread is kept to the left of the line being worked. To start, bring the needle out at 1 on the line to be worked. Go down at 2, come up at 3 (to the right of the stitch) and pull the thread through. Insert the needle at 4, holding the thread above the line with the left thumb, and come up again at 2 (in the same hole made by the previous stitch) then pull the thread through. Go down at 5, hold the loop and come up again at 4, then pull the thread through. Repeat to work a narrow line.

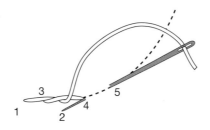

Overcast Stitch

This stitch is made up of tiny, vertical satin stitches, worked very close together over a laid thread or wire, resulting in a firm raised line. When worked over wire it gives a smooth, secure edge for cut shapes, for example, detached snowdrop petals. Place the wire along the line to be covered. Working from left to right with a stabbing motion, cover the wire with small straight stitches, pulling the thread firmly so that there are no loose stitches which may be cut when the shape is cut out.

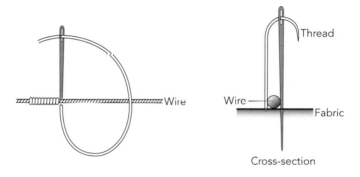

Pad Stitch

Pad stitch is used as a foundation under satin stitch when a smooth, *slightly raised* surface is required. Padding stitches can be either straight stitches or chain stitches, worked in the opposite direction to the satin stitches. Felt can replace pad stitch for a more raised effect.

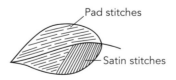

Running Stitch

See Tacking

Satin Stitch

Satin stitch is used to fill shapes such as petals or leaves. It consists of horizontal or vertical straight stitches, worked close enough together so that no fabric shows through, yet not overlapping each other. Satin stitch can be worked over a padding of felt or pad stitches. Smooth edges are easier to achieve if the shape is first outlined with split stitch (or split back stitch).

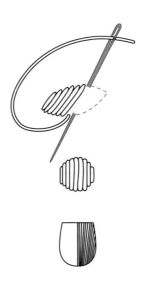

Split Stitch

Split stitch can be used either as an outline stitch or for smooth, solid fillings.
Split stitch is worked in a similar way to stem stitch; however the point of the
needle splits the preceding stitch as it is brought out of the fabric. To start, make
a straight stitch along the line to be worked. Bring the needle through to the
front, splitting the straight stitch with the point of the needle. Insert the needle
along the line then bring through to the front again to pierce the preceding stitch.
Repeat to work a narrow line of stitching, resembling fine chain stitch.

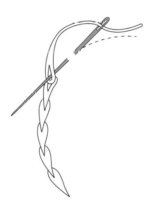

Split Back Stitch

An easier version of split stitch, especially when using one strand of thread.
Commence with a backstitch. Bring the needle out at 1, insert at 2 (splitting
the preceding stitch) and out again at 3. This results in a fine, smooth line,
ideal for stitching intricate curves.

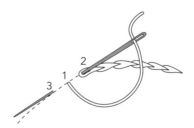

Stab Stitch

Stab stitch is used to apply leather or felt shapes to a background fabric. It consists of small straight stitches made from the background fabric over the edge of the applied shape, for example, a leather shape over felt padding. Bring the needle out at 1, and insert at 2, catching in the edge of the applied piece.

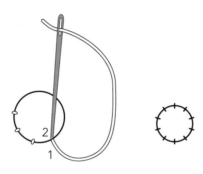

Stem Stitch

Worked from left to right, the stitches in stem stitch overlap each other to form a fine line suitable for outlines and stems. A straight (not slanted) form of stem stitch, in a stabbing motion, is ideal for stumpwork. To start, bring the needle out at 1 on the line to be worked. Go down at 2, come up at 3 and pull the thread through. Insert the needle at 4, holding the thread underneath the line with the left thumb, and come up again at 2 (sharing the hole made by the previous stitch) then pull the thread through. Go down at 5, hold the loop and come up again at 4, then pull the thread through. Repeat to work a narrow line.

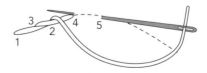

Stem Stitch Band, Raised

Stem stitch can be worked over a foundation of couched, padding thread
to produce a raised, smooth, stem stitch band, ideal for insect bodies. Lay a
preliminary foundation of padding stitches worked with soft cotton or stranded
thread. Across this padding, at fairly regular intervals, work straight (couching)
stitches at right angles to the padding thread (do not make these stitches too
tight). Then proceed to cover the padding by working rows of stem stitch over
these straight stitches, using a tapestry needle so as not to pierce the padding
thread. All the rows of stem stitch are worked in the same direction, starting
and ending either at the one point, for example, 1, or as in satin stitch, for
example, 2.

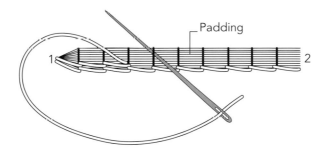

Tacking

Tacking, a dressmaking term, is a row of running stitches, longer on the top of the
fabric, used to temporarily mark an outline or to hold two pieces of fabric together.

Trellis Stitch

Trellis stitch, popular in the seventeenth century, is a needlelace filling stitch, attached only at the edges, and is most easily worked with a twisted silk thread. The first row of trellis stitch is worked into a foundation of back stitches, the size depending on the effect desired—close together and the trellis stitches resemble tent stitches in canvas work, further apart and an open 'trellis' is the result.

Bring the needle out at 1, slip it under the first back stitch (forming a 'T'—a good way to remember this stitch), pull the thread through holding the resulting loop with the left thumb. Throw the thread to the left, slip the needle through the loop (2), then pull the thread down, forming a firm knot. Repeat, to work a row of firm knots with loops in between. Insert the needle into the fabric at the end of the row.

To work a second row, bring the needle out at 3, slip the needle through the loop between two knots and pull the thread through, holding the resulting loop with the left thumb. Throw the thread to the right, slip the needle through the loop (4) then pull the thread down, forming a firm knot. Repeat to the end of the row, insert the needle and continue as above.

The rows can be worked in alternate directions as described, or in one direction only.

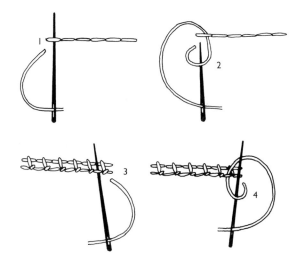

Turkey Knot

Turkey knots are worked then cut to produce a soft velvety pile. Although there are several ways to work Turkey knots, the following method works well for small areas. Use 2 strands of thread in a size 9 crewel or sharps needle. Insert the needle into the fabric at 1, holding the tail of thread with the left thumb. Come out at 2 and go down at 3 to make a *small* securing stitch. Bring the needle out again at 1 (piercing the securing stitch), pull the thread down and also hold with the left thumb.

For the next Turkey knot, insert the needle to the right at 4 (still holding the tails of thread). Come out at 5 and go down at 2 to make a small securing stitch. Bring the needle out again at 4 (piercing the securing stitch), pull the thread down and hold with the left thumb as before. Repeat to work a row.

Work each successive row directly *above* the previous row, holding all the resulting tails with the left thumb. To complete, cut all the loops, comb with an eyebrow comb, and cut the pile to the desired length. The more the pile is combed the fluffier it becomes.

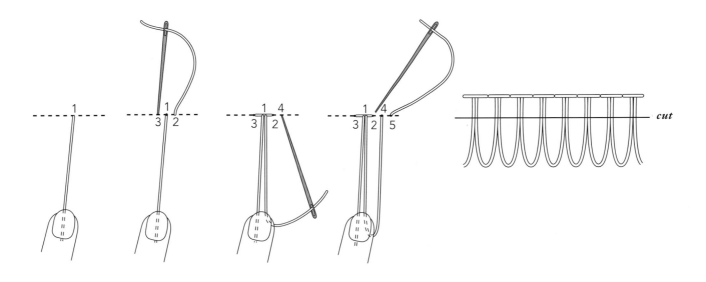

I have referred to the following for information and inspiration.

General

Beck, Thomasina. *The Embroiderers' Garden.* David & Charles, Devon, 1988.

Beck, Thomasina. *The Embroiderers' Flowers.* David & Charles, Devon, 1992.

Benn, Elizabeth. *Treasures from the Embroiderers' Guild Collection.* David & Charles, Devon, 1991.

Bilimoff, Michèle. *Promenade dans des Jardins Disparus.* Éditions Ouest-France, Rennes, 2001.

Carey, Jacqui. *Elizabethan Stitches.* Carey Company, Devon, 2012.

Cole, H. *Heraldry Decoration & Floral Forms.* Crescent Books, New York, 1988.

de Gex, Jenny. *Shakespeare's Flowers.* Pavilion Books, London, 1994.

de Gex, Jenny. *Bible Flowers.* Harmony Books, London, 1996.

Digby, George Wingfield. *Elizabethan Embroidery.* Faber & Faber, London, 1963.

Dyer, T. F. Thistleton. *Folk-Lore of Shakespeare.* 1883.

Fisher, Celia. *Flowers in Medieval Manuscripts.* The British Library, London, 2004.

Fisher, Celia. *The Medieval Flower Book.* The British Library, London, 2007.

Hobhouse, Penelope. *Plants in Garden History.* Pavilion Books, London, 1992.

Holmes, Martin. *Proud Northern Lady.* Phillimore, West Sussex, 2005.

Innes, Miranda & Perry, Clay. *Medieval Flowers.* Kyle Cathie Ltd, London, 1997.

Kerr, Jessica. *Shakespeare's Flowers.* Longman, London, 1969.

King, D. & Levy, S. *Embroidery in Britain from 1200 to 1750.* V & A Museum, London, 1993.

Kingsbury, Noël. *The Wild Flower Garden.* Conran Octopus, London, 1994.

Landsberg, Sylvia. *The Medieval Garden.* British Museum Press, London, 1995.

Martin, W. Keble. *The Concise British Flora in Colour.* Ebury Press, London, 1965.

Pickles, Sheila. *The Language of Wild Flowers.* Pavilion Books, London, 1995.

Powell, Claire. *The Meaning of Flowers.* Jupiter Books, London, 1977.

Shorleyker, Richard. *A Schole-House for the Needle.* RJL Smith & Associates, Shropshire, 1998.

Synge, Lanto. *Art of Embroidery*. Antique Collectors' Club, Woodbridge, 2001.

Vickery, Roy. *Oxford Dictionary of Plant-Lore*. Oxford University Press, Oxford, 1995.

Ware, D. & Stafford, M. *An Illustrated Dictionary of Ornament*. Allen & Unwin, London, 1974.

Watkins, Susan. *Elizabeth I and her World*. Thames & Hudson, 1998.

Woodward, Marcus. *Leaves from Gerard's Herball*. Dover Publications, New York, 1969.

Embroidery

Christie, Grace. *Samplers and Stitches*. Batsford, London, 1920.

Enthoven, Jacqueline. *The Stitches of Creative Embroidery*. Reinhold Publishing, New York, 1964.

Thomas, Mary. *Dictionary of Embroidery Stitches*. Hodder & Stoughton, London, 1934.

Stumpwork

Nicholas, Jane. *Stumpwork Embroidery: A Collection of Fruits, Flowers, Insects*. Milner, Australia, 1995.

Nicholas, Jane. *Stumpwork Embroidery: Designs and Projects*. Milner, Australia, 1998.

Nicholas, Jane. *Stumpwork Dragonflies*. Milner, Australia, 2000.

Nicholas, Jane. *Stumpwork, Goldwork & Surface Embroidery Beetle Collection*. Milner, Australia, 2004.

Nicholas, Jane. *The Complete Book of Stumpwork Embroidery*. Milner, Australia, 2005.

Nicholas, Jane. *Stumpwork Medieval Flora*. Milner, Australia, 2009.

Nicholas, Jane. *Stumpwork Embroidery—Turkish, Syrian and Persian Tiles*. Milner, Australia, 2010.

Nicholas, Jane. *Stumpwork Butterflies & Moths*. Milner, Australia, 2013.

Top: **Primrose border from Miss Higgin's Handbook of Embroidery** *(1912)*

Title page:, Endpapers: Embroidered satin coverlet, English, early 17th century. Image taken from Cole, H. *Heraldry Decoration and Floral Forms.* Crescent Books, New York, 1988 (p. 242)

Page 6, 7, 14: Elizabethan sleeve-panel in blackwork; held in the Royal Scottish Museum, Edinburgh. © National Museums Scotland.

Page 9: A plan for a typical manor-house garden in England, from William Lawson's *New Orchard and Garden*, published in 1618. Image taken from Hobhouse, P. *Plants in Garden History.* Pavilion Books, London, 1992 (p. 105)

Page 11: The title page of John Gerard's *The Herball or Generall Historie of Plantes,* published in 1597. Image taken from Watkins, Susan. *Elizabeth I and her World.* Thames & Hudson, 1998 (p. 111)

Page 27: A Cornflower drawn by Grace Christie, from *Needle and Thread* (1914). Image taken from Beck, Thomasina. *The Embroiderer's Flowers.* David & Charles, Devon, 1992 (p. 125)

Page 30: A Rose embroidery motif (John Overton). Image taken from Beck, Thomasina. *The Embroiderer's Flowers.* David & Charles, Devon, 1992 (p. 40)

Page 31: *Rosa gallica* by Pierre-Joseph Redouté (1759–1840). Image taken from WikiCommons.

Page 37: Borage designs from: (a) slip for a cushion (c.1600); (b) transfer pattern in *The Embroidress* (1930s). Images taken from Beck, Thomasina. *The Embroiderer's Flowers.* David & Charles, Devon, 1992 (p. 66)

Page 52: Barberry embroidery motifs. Images taken from Shorleyker, Richard. *A Schole-house for the Needle.* RJL Smith, Shropshire, 1998 (pp. N1, N2)

Page 56: A carnation embroidery motif (John Overton). Image taken from Beck, Thomasina. *The Embroiderer's Flowers.* David & Charles, Devon, 1992 (p. 40)

Page 57 : Gillyflower embroidery motif . Image taken from Shorleyker, Richard. *A Schole-house for the Needle.* RJL Smith, Shropshire, 1998 (p. Q1)

Page 62: Strawberry embroidery motifs. Shorleyker, Richard. *A Schole-house for the Needle*. RJL Smith, Shropshire, 1998 (pp. N1, N2)

Pages 68, 77: Knapweed and cornflower types. Images taken from Cole, H. *Heraldry Decoration and Floral Forms*. Crescent Books, New York, 1988 (p. 141)

Page 73: Bullaces and other wild plums. *Bourdichon Hours*, French, early 16th century.© British Library Board, London, Add. 18855, f.43

Page 77: A cornflower, drawn by Grace Christie, from *Needle and Thread* (1914). Image taken from Beck, Thomasina. *The Embroiderer's Flowers*. David & Charles, Devon, 1992 (p. 125)

Page 99: Sweet briar embroidery motif (John Overton). Image taken from Beck, Thomasina. *The Embroiderer's Flowers*. David & Charles, Devon, 1992 (p. 40)

Page 142: Embroidered panel, possibly from a coif, English, early 17th century. The Embroiderers' Guild Collection, London; Accession Number: EG 1982.79. Benn, E. *Treasures from the Embroiderers' Guild Collection*. David & Charles, Devon, 1991 (p. 15)

Page 143: Embroidered coif, English, early 17th century. The Embroiderers' Guild Collection, London; Accession Number: EG 161. Image taken from Benn, E. *Treasures from the Embroiderers' Guild Collection*. David & Charles, 1991 (p. 14)

Pages 154, 155: Pea pods embroidery motifs. Images taken from Shorleyker, Richard. *A Schole-house for the Needle*. RJL Smith, Shropshire, 1998 (pp. N2, N3)

Page 173, 267: Primrose border from *Miss Higgin's Handbook of Embroidery* (1912). Image taken from Beck, Thomasina. *The Embroiderer's Garden*. David & Charles, Devon, 1988 (p. 122)

Page 178: Honeysuckle embroidery motif. Image taken from Shorleyker, Richard. *A Schole-house for the Needle*. RJL Smith, Shropshire, 1998 (p. Q1)

Page 179: Honeysuckle embroidery motif. Image taken from Beck, Thomasina. *The Embroiderer's Flowers*. David & Charles, Devon, 1992 (p. 40)

Page 184: Rose embroidery motif (John Overton). Image taken from Beck, Thomasina. *The Embroiderer's Flowers*. David & Charles, Devon, 1992 (p. 40)

Page 184: Page 31: *Rosa gallica* by Pierre-Joseph Redouté (1759–1840). Image taken from WikiCommons.

Page 185: Rose design from *The Craftsman's Plant Book* by Ralph Hatton (1909). Image taken from Beck, Thomasina. *The Embroiderer's Garden*. David & Charles, Devon, 1988 (p. 9)

Page 186: Forms of heraldic Tudor rose. © *Illustrated Dictionary of Ornament*, Ware & Stafford (p. 183)

Page 187: Finest example of embroidered book cover in existence. The Bodleian Library, Oxford; Accession Number: Douce Bib. Eng. 1583 b.1. Image taken from Watkins, S. *Elizabeth I and her World*. Thames & Hudson, 1998 (p. 153)

Page 192: Bluebell embroidery motif (John Overton). Beck, Thomasina. *The Embroiderer's Flowers*. David & Charles, Devon, 1992 (p. 40)

Pages 204, 208: Daisy illustrations from MS Ashmole 1504, Bodleian Library, Oxford (Folios 7 & 7v). Images taken from de Gex, Jenny. *Shakespeare's Flowers*. Pavilion Books, London, 1994 (pp. 29, 28)

Page 212: Daisy embroidery motif (John Overton). Image taken from Beck, Thomasina. *The Embroiderer's Flowers*. David & Charles, Devon, 1992 (p. 40)

Page 213: Designs for daisies by Jacques de Moyne de Morgues (1586) and Joan Drew (1929). Images taken from Beck, Thomasina. *The Embroiderer's Flowers*. David & Charles, Devon, 1992 (p. 7)

Additional images supplied by Shutterstock

ACKNOWLEDGEMENTS

I would like to extend my gratitude to all those people who continue to share their passion for stumpwork with me. Whether by correspondence or in class, your enthusiasm provides invaluable motivation.

My wonderful family continues to provide wholehearted support and encouragement for my work. Special thanks to John, who makes all the kits and runs the mail order service with amazing efficiency and attention to detail.

My thanks to Phillipa Turnbull, for introducing me to Lady Anne Clifford and the charming town of Appleby-in-Westmoreland. Many happy memories and much inspiration.

Sincere thanks to my dear sewing friends for their companionship and the opportunity to share ideas and cherished stitching time.

Finally, to all those involved in the production of this book at Sally Milner Publishing—your expertise, and belief in my work, is sincerely appreciated.

SUPPLIES & KITS

The threads, beads and needlework products referred to in this book are available from Jane Nicholas Embroidery and specialist needlework shops.

A mail order service is offered by Jane Nicholas Embroidery. Visit the website and view the entire range of stumpwork kits, books and embroidery supplies including wires, fabrics, leather, beads, hoops, needles and scissors. Thread ranges include Au Ver à Soie, Cifonda, chenille, DMC, Kreinik, Madeira and YLI, and goldwork supplies. Framecraft brooches, boxes and paperweights are stocked for finishing.

Jane Nicholas Embroidery
P.O. Box 300
BOWRAL N.S.W. 2576
AUSTRALIA

Tel: +61 2 4861 1175
Fax: +61 2 4861 1175
Email: jane@janenicholas.com
Web: www.janenicholas.com

About the Author

Jane Nicholas has been researching and working in the field of embroidery for over twenty years. Specialising in stumpwork and goldwork embroidery, she has written eight books and has contributed widely to journals and magazines on the subject.

In 1999 Jane was awarded a Churchill Fellowship to further her studies in stumpwork in the United Kingdom and in 2005 was awarded the Order of Australia Medal (OAM), for her 'services to hand embroidery as an artist, teacher and author'.

She teaches widely in Australia, New Zealand and the United States of America and continues to research and develop new techniques—particularly in stumpwork. A separate, but often related, area of her work is as a maker of artists' books and boxes.